1003589676

WITHIN THE HEARTS AND MINDS OF PRISONERS

	DATE DUE	

LEARNING RESOURCE
CENTRE
GRANT MacEWAN
COMMUNITY COLLEGE

ABOUT THE AUTHOR

Edward M. Scott has had a variety of academic and clinical appointments, some of which are the following: state mental hospital chief psychologist; clinical director of an alcohol and drug center; consultant for a school for delinquent girls; guest lecturer for the Utah Summer School for Alcoholism; and therapist for offenders in and out of prison.

He has authored three books, edited a fourth book with his wife Kathy, and co-authored a fifth book with Dr. George Palermo. Over seventy-five articles of his have appeared in a variety of professional journals. For fourteen years, he was editor of the *International Journal of Offender Therapy and Comparative Criminology*. He presently is an editorial consultant for *Psychotherapy*.

At Oregon Health Sciences University (OHSU) he has held the rank of professor of psychiatry and presently he is a professor emeritus of psychiatry.

WITHIN THE HEARTS AND MINDS OF PRISONERS

An In-Depth View of Prisoners in Therapy

By

EDWARD M. SCOTT, PH.D.

Professor Emeritus of Psychiatry
Oregon Health Sciences University

Editor Emeritus of International Journal of
Offender Therapy and Comparative Criminology
Certified Group Psychotherapist

CHARLES C THOMAS • PUBLISHER, LTD.
Springfield • Illinois • U.S.A.

Published and Distributed Throughout the World by

CHARLES C THOMAS • PUBLISHER, LTD.
2600 South First Street
Springfield, Illinois 62794-9265

This book is protected by copyright. No part of
it may be reproduced in any manner without
written permission from the publisher.

©1998 by CHARLES C THOMAS • PUBLISHER, LTD.
ISBN 0-398-06876-3 (cloth)
ISBN 0-398-06877-1 (paper)

Library of Congress Catalog Card Number: 98-18638

With THOMAS BOOKS careful attention is given to all details of manufacturing and design. It is the Publisher's desire to present books that are satisfactory as to their physical qualities and artistic possibilities and appropriate for their particular use. THOMAS BOOKS will be true to those laws of quality that assure a good name and good will.

Printed in the United States of America
MS-R-3

Library of Congress Cataloging in Publication Data

Scott, Edward M.
    Within the hearts and minds of prisoners : an in-depth view of prisoners in therapy / by Edward M. Scott.
      p.   cm.
    Includes bibliographical references and index.
    ISBN 0-398-06876-3 (cloth) . -- ISBN 0-398-06877-1 (pbk.)
    1. Prisoners--Mental Health. 2. Prisoners--Mental Health services 3. Correctional psychology. 4. Prisoners--Counseling of. 5. Psychotherapy. 6. Fairy tales--Therapeutic use. I. Title.
RC451.4.P68S36   1998
616.89'14'086927--dc21
                                                      98-18638
                                                         CIP

To
My lovely wife and best friend
Kathy

and to our adult children who have enriched our lives
Kathleen Hollingsworth
Mike Scott
Maureen Miller
Tim Scott
Molly Pellessier

FOREWORD

Perhaps the loneliest person in prison is the prison psychologist. Dr. Edward Scott's impassioned story of his thousands of days and nights as a prison psychologist and group therapist are impeccably profiled in *Within The Hearts and Minds of Prisoners*. The most telling fact of the predicament of the prison psychologist is found in the irony that the American Group Psychotherapy Association has only recently included prison group therapy in its annual meetings. As with the prison itself, counseling and psychological services to both staff and inmates continue to struggle for legitimacy in professional research and professional standards of performance.

It is said that the prison defines the people in it - both the keeper and the kept - but this simple idiom is incapable of defining the true interactive spirit behind the walls. The layered psychosocial efforts of pure survival, measured in incremental but heroic dimensions of self-will, self-discovery, self-encounter, and confrontation on both sides of the bars speaks of the real nature and character of the prison in mass society. The many niches of humanity in the house of darkness, as epitomized in the rare empathetic prison-life films *Fortune in Mens Eyes* (1979) and *The Shawshank Redemption* (1994), confirm a classic thesis of prison as a place of psychological cleansing and discovery of epochal proportions (e.g., Malcolm X, Nelson Mandela, Anwar Sadat, Victor Frankl). While one can draw a profile of the typical criminal, it is more than likely that most offenders will fall outside of that profile. What they have in common and what separates them from people who have not been caught up in the criminal justice system is the unique experience of losing their freedom. They have all, at one time in their lives, been stripped of their possessions and lived in an institution where their daily activity was governed by the needs of the facility and not their own desires. Their relationships with their families and friends were broken or severely strained, and their sense of self-respect and dignity were greatly diminished.

For some, institutionalization is a traumatic hell, in which suicide or an attempt at escape is strong consideration. For others, prison is a welcome relief from the stresses of using drugs and living in the streets. But for all, I believe, prison creates a deep hunger for all that cannot be had and a thirst for self-respect and dignity. If, upon release from prison, a person is not prepared to secure work and be self-supporting, his return to prison is almost inevitable. Without work, his self-respect cannot be restored and his life is without dignity. Repeatedly, ex-offenders have confirmed that it was only within the distilled atmosphere of forced, positive peer-interactive group therapy and counseling sessions that the seedbed for change was discovered.

Dr. Edward Scott enables the voices from within to have a fulfilled listening. The professional struggles of prison psychologists and the pathos of inmate actors, sealed in a shellac of pathetic solipsism, fear, paranoia, rage, pride, disgust, guilt, and desire for redemption, peel away in this cataloguing and revelation of the peer counseling dynamic. Taut in racial polemics and yielding in a common human bondage of the psychological-pain of separation, the intrinsic dynamics of these unique counseling sessions are vividly portrayed. The peculiar emotional insulation as an essential garment of the professional psychologist in both the clinical and academic realms is a driving force throughout this book. The reader is constantly connected with the crucial capabilities of the prison psychologist for nurturing and protecting the essential elan vital of these group sessions. Often bearing the brunt of group-and-individual anger and hate, the psychologist is at any moment the target of racism, target of surrogate parental/familial rage, an alienated agent of the system, or simply a "dirty old man" interested in prurient stories of sex and intrigue.

To the outsider, the cynicism, clowning, and venom embodied in the typical prison group therapy session may seem deceptive, but the skilled correctional psychologist readily sees beneath this hard but thin veneer of alienation a cry for meaning... for congruence...the desire to be part of the family of man. In the central chapters of this unique book, Scott guides us through the proverbial forest of suicides haunting criminal offenders.

Is there a criminal mind? Yes, is the unequivocal answer proffered by Scott. It is a state of mind that rides on the typical convict mentality that "I'm riding a bum beef." For Dr. Edward Scott, this mind-set is a spur for beginning a provocative and successful mode of psychological encounter and rehabilitative change. Through the skillful use of simple but intrinsically vivid exercises, Scott presents his prisoner-patients with the assignment of answering the engaging question: What is in your Heart and Mind? This process continues throughout this book, combining prisoner stories as a cup for the broken vessel of love for troubled minds. *Eros and Agape*...disconcerting, yes, in the initial read; deeply confirming in the comparative analysis of the psychological testing field (Chapter 4) including Toch's Prison Preference Inventory (PPI) and Scott's unique Prison Expression Test (PET). The problem of remembering earlier life's experiences, framed in either good (positive) or bad (negative) is integral to Scott's earlier work with children (5-6 grades), high school students, alcoholics, mental patients and normal individuals.

Through the PET, developed in part as a modus operandi of maximizing the rich milieu of psychological insights garnered from his use of fairy tales: prisoners' replies, prisoners' stories from blank pages, and prisoners' drawings, Scott reveals a fascinating and affirming common bond for psychological healing. Chapter 10 presents PTSD (Post Traumatic Stress Disorder) vs PGE (Post Growth Experience) offering a new concept for psychological and emotional health that provides a needed extension (and relief) from the APA's modern buzz word: *post traumatic stress disorder.* This new concept presents an elucidating and valuable discussion for the growing number psychologists, counselors, and professional correctional officers in the penal enterprise. The pragmatism of the Prison Expression Test (PET) and its linkage to Post Growth Experience (PGE) is seen as enabling both a voice and ear for the inmate in counseling and the therapist as a prison professional in the larger context of understaffed and overcrowded prisons. The reader will revisit Chapter 11, Reflections and Suggestions, numerous times. It is in these closing pages that Dr. Scott provides meaning for us all in the purpose and place of psychological services and group therapy in prison. With a beautiful and concise depiction of the "crystallization of discontent," often expressed in a wide variety of group therapy sessions as "*sick and tired of being sick and tired,*" Scott offers up a gentle and creative thesis.

It is still considered taboo for professional psychologists to indulge in the legitimation of "love and sexual behavior" as simple roles of psychological being. Sagarin (1980) highlights the risks involved in the manifestations of taboos in criminology:

> All sciences, the physical as well as the social, have areas in which one must tread lightly, aware that something, whether can of worms or Pandora's box, is

about to be opened and that the world is not ready to cope with the possible or foreseeable consequences. In criminology, it appears that a number of views —rather than subjects—have become increasingly delicate and sensitive, as if all those who espouse them were inherently evil, or at least stupidly insensitive to the consequences of their research. Thus, it takes courage to say what some of the proponents of unpopular views have said, or it takes unawareness of the logic of the position, or both. One cannot always be sure.

Dr. Edward Scott is sure. As he has done throughout his remarkable and giving career, Dr. Scott closes his book by giving to convicts a voice on the subject of love. By this simple act, he reaffirms that love is implanted in life, is unconditionally identified with it. It is in this mode that correctional psychologist and inmate-patient can find common ground.

Jess Maghan, Ph.D.

References

Garland, D.: *Punishment in Modern Society: A Study in Social Theory,* Chicago: The University of Chicago Press, 1990.

Jacobs, J.: The Limits of Racial Integration. In James B. Jacobs (Ed.): *New Perspectives on Prisons and Imprisonment.* Ithaca: Cornell University Press, 1983. Reprinted from *Criminal Law Bulletin, 18* (2) March/April 1982: 117-53.

Mair, G.: What Works - Nothing or Everything? Measuring Effectiveness in Sentences? *HM Prison Service: Research Bulletin, 30:* 3-8, 1991.

Morrison, W.: Modernity, Imprisonment, and Social Solidarity. In Roger Matthews & Peter Francis (Eds.): *Prison 2000, An International Perspective on the Current State and Future of Imprisonment.* New York: St. Martins Press, 1996, pp. 219-239.

Sagarin, E.: *Taboos in Criminology.* Beverly Hills: Sage Publications, 1980.

(Dr. Jess Maghan is the Director of the Forum for Comparative Corrections and the Center for Research in Law and Justice at the University of Illinois at Chicago. He has promoted programs in prison staff development in Eastern Europe, South Africa, and the Peoples Republic of China by working with prison officials and inmates.)

INTRODUCTORY NOTE

Professor Edward Scott, in this book, offers the reader a view of his broad experience as a group psychotherapist with criminal offenders. He conducts the reader on a lengthy and interesting group psychotherapeutic journey. With easiness and by the use of confrontation mythology, he assists the prisoners to relive some of the their forgotten experiences and provides the reader the experience of being present during the group sessions. The central focus of his therapy sessions is that of stories, narratives and anecdotes, as well as "stories within the stories"–those often impromptu stories of the prisoners–loaded with affects of the heart or "bare-fact" memories. He employs the messages found in fairy tales, the prisoners' reactions to a blank page, or their interpretations of vignettes produced by the prisoners themselves in an effort to liberate the inner thoughts and emotions from these violent offenders. This in-depth material many have believed to be unreachable. Obviously, we are not given all the details of these sessions, but rather the highlights. These are highly interesting, especially Dr. Scott's "to-the-point" interpretations of them. He is a professional with compassion, but reality-oriented. Dr. Scott demonstrates a vast knowledge of the psychology of the prisoners. His frequent referrals to pertinent literature arising during interactive group psychotherapy sessions are truly enlightening.

Through the establishment of a good therapeutic alliance with the group members, Dr. Scott's humanness transfuses them with self-confidence. The reader has the clear perception that their participation becomes not only spontaneous, but they have a significant lead during the discussions. This is actually what he wants. Dr. Scott seems to be able to enliven the prisoners in a psychological sense. It is clear that Dr. Scott regards their comments as important. The lid of their Pandora's box is gently opened with Dr. Scott's nonintrusive but supportive help. Particularly, the fairy tales written by the prisoners are striking. Some seem to be the product of experienced writers, capable of juggling symbols with extreme dexterity and to express wishes, regrets, grandiosity, hostility, insight and, as is usually the case with offenders, good hindsight in judgment.

Dr. Scott is a good listener and a man of erudition, able to put his vast knowledge of humanity to good use. His method is indirect but engaging and based on common sense without the mumbo-jumbo at times found in psychological jargon. Interestingly, the members of his groups are quite responsive to his basic reality-oriented therapy, even though insight-gaining comes from the stimuli of mythological stories or fairy tales. He is successful in making the offenders introspective, expressive, and reflective. Perhaps his success is due to the fact that he does not use the usual cold, sterile projective testing materials but these archetypical stories that, part of humanity's collective unconscious, are easily understood even by the noninitiated.

The book should be read and attentively studied by all those involved in working with offenders within the carceral (prison) system.

GEORGE B. PALERMO, M.D.
Clinical Professor of Psychiatry and Neurology,
Director of Criminological Psychiatry
Department of Psychiatry
Medical College of Wisconsin
Milwaukee, Wisconsin

PREFACE

This book has the focus of revealing the emotional and intellectual lives of prisoners based on weekly contacts with them. Some of the contacts were for a year. The majority of the contacts were about six months duration. Typical of any human relationship, periodic contacts over a period of time are far superior to a brief encounter or to either an evaluation or psychological testing. The extended contact assures that not only defenses and defects will emerge, *but as important,* the individual will mature if an opportunity is provided. This, I believe, is the sine qua non of any real treatment program or of any relationship.

The modality utilized was that of weekly group therapy sessions. Open exchange between the prisoners and with the therapist was the fundamental dynamic. The basic rule was: "No psychiatric swearing." This meant that the prisoner could not say "I don't know" for any question. Hence, an inner search was demanded which in turn loosened both emotional and intellectual stances.

Specific topics, themes, and assumptions were not only questioned but were explored: traumatic vs growth-promoting experiences; looking into one's heart (emotional life); creation of fairy tales; playfulness; human horror; love and sex. The latter (sex) was formulated in the form of a question: "Imagine the moment of your conception."

The above approaches yielded a rich and varied harvest from my prisoner patients. Hopefully the reader, whether lay or professional, of *Within the Hearts and Minds of Prisoners* will gather significant data to counter the misinformed cliches currently circulating regarding prisoners.

In brief, this book rewards the educated reader who wants more than pop-psychology, teddy bear sociology, or nothing-works criminology.

ACKNOWLEDGMENTS

The author recognizes the very expert assistance provided by Michael Payne Thomas of Charles C Thomas, Publisher, and his entire staff who so effectively contributed to the completion of this book.

To those prison patients who were members of my various group psychotherapy sessions, I owe a debt of gratitude. I gladly and thankfully acknowledge their efforts.

On a personal and professional basis, the author needs to thank a former mentor, John Waterman, M.D. Dr. Waterman was a clinical mentor for all seasons and for all cases. To Joe Bloom, M.D., a thanks for his encouragement and support when he was Chair of the Department of Psychiatry and presently Dean of the School of Medicine at the Oregon Health Sciences University. Ron Turco, M.D., a friend and colleague for many years, I must thank for his devotion to endless study and his practical mentorship on conducting a forensic evaluation. From Dale Mortimer, M.D. (a bright young psychiatrist), the author grew to appreciate the role and nonrole of medication with prisoners.

Bill Wheeler, B.A., and presently a candidate for a master's degree, as a former prison guard (big and husky), demonstrated time and time again how to combine the skills of sterness and effective kindness. He was a much gifted mentor in the prison trenches–where few exist. To him I say, "Thanks, Bill."

My wife, Kathy, has been a constant and positive influence for writing this book, while on a very practical level she gave willingly and generously of her editorial skills. To complete the list of those who helped with editing, I need to note that my granddaughter, Katie Hollingworth, a seventeen-year-old "eagle-eyed" whiz, caught many of her grandfather's mistakes.

Finally, to Mrs. Virginia Micciche who was able to read the manuscript from my handwritten pages through its many versions until completion, a sincere thanks.

CONTENTS

Page

Foreword–Jess Maghan vii
Introductory Note–George Palermo xi
Preface xiii

Chapter

1. INTRODUCTION 3
   Human Horror 4
   Creativity 5
   The Narrative Self 6
2. WHAT'S IN YOUR HEART AND MIND? 9
   Working Alliance 10
   Descriptions of the Heart's Function 10
   Groups' Responses 12
   Three Prisoner Vignettes 16
   The Prisoner and the World 19
3. THE BRAIN AND LOVE? 23
   Eros vs Agape 24
   Kardia and Its Various Meanings 24
   Biological vs Social Aspects of the Brain 26
   Prisoner Vignette: "What's at the Bottom of My Heart" 28
   Evil 30
   Altered State of Consciousness: A New Entry–Evil 31
4. PRISONERS' EXPRESSION TEST (PET) 33
   Construction of the PET 34
   Research Results of the PET 34
   A Prisoner's Response to Question 49, "I Manipulate" 43
5. FAIRY TALES: PRISONERS' REPLIES 45
   German Word Maeve Means Message 46

Prisoner Responses To: "Are You Real or Mechanical?" ... 48
The Fisherman and the Genie: Prolonged
   Imprisonment Increases Hatred? 56
Prisoner Responses 56
Bettelheim's Thesis: Partly Failed 59
Reflections 59

6: FAIRY TALES BY PRISONERS 61
   Fairy Tale 1: The Tale of Anak the Giant and the Sylph ... 61
   Reflection 63
   Fairy Tale 2: The Little Pony 64
   Reflection 67
   Fairy Tale 3: The Time Machine 68
   Reflection 68
   Fairy Tale 4: A Modern Don Quixote 69
   Reflection 70
   Fairy Tale 5: All Music: A Replacement of the Magic Flute? 71
   Reflection 72
   Fairy Tale 6: Little Red Riding Hood: The True Story as
      Told by the Wolf 73
   Reflection 75
   Inspired Fiction?: by Bill and Ted 75

7: STORIES FROM A BLANK PAGE 79
   Final Stage: Stories From a Blank Page 79
   Stories 80
   Reflections 87

8. FOR PRISONERS: SEX IN THE KEY OF C 91
   Biblical and Gilgamesh Background 92
   Three Drawings by the Same Prisoner 95
   What Do You Know About the Moment/Time of
      Your Conception? 97
   Reflections 100

9. GROUP PSYCHOTHERAPY 103
   Introduction 103
   A Polysemous Thesis 104
   Some Historical Notes Regarding Group Psychotherapy .. 105

Contents

     My Prisoner Groups' Reactions to Zimbardo's
        Simulation of Prison 106
     Basic Group Psychotherapy Organization, Techniques,
        and Examples of Clinical Material 108
     Some Advanced Group Psychotherapy Techniques
        and Orientation 111
     Symbolism and Reality 112
     Reflection 113
     Art Work 114
     True Play and Playfulness Lacking in Prisoners 116
10. PTSD VS PGE 121
     PGE Question Responses 123
     A PTSD Memory by a Prisoner 126
     Some Research on Memory 128
     Prisoner Response to Maslow's Thesis 130
     Reflections 133
     PGE: A New Concept 133
11. REFLECTIONS AND SUGGESTIONS 135
     Propositions 135
     Treatment 135
     Personality Change? 137
     Evil 141
     Creativity 144
     Love 145
     Prisoners and Their Relation to the World 145
     A Proposed Course for Prisoners 147

Appendix I 149
Appendix II 156
References 159
Author Index 165
Subject Index 167

WITHIN THE HEARTS AND MINDS OF PRISONERS

Chapter 1

INTRODUCTION

E.B. White (1977) has reflected, "Only a person who is congenitally self-centered has the effrontery and the stamina to write essays" (p. viii). The therapist who works with offenders either in or out of prison for any length of time requires stamina and a degree of effrontery. The former (stamina) is necessary due to reports, typically negative, regarding the statistical success of therapeutic efforts with offenders. It is considerably easier and "cleaner" to conduct some type of research project on offenders. "Cleaner" suggests lack of face-to-face or continued involvement with the offender. The latter (effrontery) indicates the give and take of ongoing interaction. Therapists with a prima-donna personality do not survive.

Another variable needs to be added—not for the essayist—but for the long-time therapist with offenders. Specifically, I mean bitterness and feelings of defeat. The present author has been practicing therapy with offenders in and out of prison for a period of more than twenty years. My experience and my reflections are unlike those of Halleck. Halleck (1968), a psychiatrist, had argued, "Where psychotherapy has been attempted with criminals it has yielded encouraging results" (p. 201). Years later, when no longer a prison therapist, Halleck (1971) stated, "Now I am plagued with the doubt as to whether I behaved morally in carrying out psychotherapy in prison at all" (p. 30). My experience is just the opposite—the more I practiced therapy in prison the more effective it appeared.

HUMAN HORROR

Farley (1996), recent past president of the APA (American Psychological Association), stated, "Nothing eludes our scholarship and science like the roots of human horror. If psychology cannot help understand and reduce human horror, we will have failed our original promise. At the moment, we stand very close to being a discipline concerned with relatively superficial problems: the anxieties and fears of otherwise healthy people (how's my self-esteem today?)" (p. 775).

This book "takes on" some of the horrors of humankind. In brief, this book is not written for beginners who work with offenders. Rather, it assumes by analogy that the reader has climbed some of the easier mountains of working with offenders. Said differently, the book takes for granted that the reader has had courses in abnormal psychology, criminology, supervised counseling and personality development, and personality disorders. DSM-IV (1994) should be familiar, particularly Axis II. These are the basic tools needed to climb the higher mountains of face-to-face encounters with prisoners who are angry, depressed, and have others–especially you–to blame for their current difficulties.

What added "tools" does this book offer? In a recent book, *The Paranoid: In and Out of Prison*, by Palmero and Scott (1997), the latter author provided some basic tools for the climbing of higher mountains with prisoners. In this book, advanced "tools" (methods) are indicated. First, it describes a useful and usable practical psychological instrument for assessing each prisoner before you take him on the "high climb." After years of using other psychological tests, which I found not too helpful, I developed the PET (Prisoner's Expression Test). This test provides the therapist with both a varied and in-depth evaluation. If poorly done, refusal to take him with you and other prisoner "high-climbers" would be a wise decision.

This book's title, *Inside the Hearts and Minds of Prisoners*, is the focus of two chapters, one clinical and one academic. This is an attempt to unite, not separate, these two approaches.

A perennial "visitor" in this work is that of sex. In the chapter entitled, "Sex in the Key of C," the reader will find an entirely new approach. It opened some painful and troubling material. I was told, "You're a dirty old man," because of this approach, by two prisoners, one in for murder, the other in for rape.

An even more frequent "visitor" than sex was that of being a victim. To use their terms, all were "riding a bum beef." Several attempts were made to confront this self-selected diagnosis. It is a type of diagnosis which provides with it rights, the rights of getting even. Years ago, Scott (1971), in his book *An Arena for Happiness*, found that patient groups (alcoholics and psychiatric patients) judged that their lives were not as happy as "normal" people. The chapter "PTSD (Post Traumatic Stress Disorder) vs PGE (Post Growth Experience)" was an effort to assess prisoners' self-judgement regarding happiness.

CREATIVITY

Sternberg and Lubart (1996) have called attention to their review of Psychological Abstracts from 1975 to 1994, "that approximately one-half of one percent . . . concerned creativity" (p. 678). I am especially pleased with the chapter "Fairy Tales by Prisoners." That particular chapter, I believe, is unique in the professional literature regarding prisoners. It had been decided that a "pump-primer" would be necessary. That was the motive for the chapter "Fairy Tales: Prisoners' Replies."

One of the clinical messages I hope becomes recognizable is that of responding to the good (mature, productive, inquisitive, etc.) efforts of my prison groups. This, in my opinion, is a type of healing. I am, however, not a "positive-patsy" type of therapist. Anna Freud (1985) has stated, "If you haven't built the house, you can't throw somebody out of it" (p. 238). She meant that some structure of personality is required to resist immediate gratification. I want to extend Anna Freud's analogy. Prisoners (most) have not built their own house, but they willingly enter (uninvited) another's house or heart.

The idea of mountain climbing, suggested earlier, provides a therapeutic opportunity for each climber to gain skills. The instructor (therapist) can point out, at times demonstrate, but he can't do it for the prisoner. One of the significant advantages of group therapy is to have one or more of the prisoners observe another prisoner's attempts and often success at a particular skill. A nearly perfect example is that of "being a stand-up-man"—not to others, but to the self. A "rewriting" (verbally) of old worn-out stories is often what happened.

This leads into the area of stories. According to standard dictionaries, a story may be true or untrue. A narrative is a more formal term and indicates that the material is true; whereas, an anecdote is a short account, personal and at times entertaining.

THE NARRATIVE SELF

Authors regarding the above indicate no consistent pattern. For example, Coles (1989), a renowned author and psychiatrist, has a book entitled *The Call of Stories*. Coles was deeply impressed when one of his clinical supervisors insisted, "The people who come to see us bring us their stories" (p. 7). The same supervisor (Ludwig) commented that the therapist must be able "to interpret their stories correctly" (p. 7).

A research team, Zeanah et al. (1989), in their descriptions of various stages of the self, named the fifth stage "The Narrative Self." They attempted to explain this stage by having written it as a "new domain of experience that constructs a story from a variety of elements (e.g., actor, action, intention, instrumentality, and context) drawn from the other senses of the self" (p. 662). Furthermore, these authors suggested that "this history becomes the life story that an adult patient initially presents to a therapist" (p. 662). Note the interchange of narrative, story, and history.

Spence (1984) has provided an important distinction in his text regarding narrative truth and historical truth. Vitz (1990), in his article "The Use of Stories in Moral Development," has provided an excellent summary of the professional literature. Rennie (1994) has indicated a crucial role of storytelling for patients.

Anecdote is from the Greek: *an*=not; *ekotos*=out; hence, unknown. Dunne (1973) has held that, "There are stories within stories" (p. 2). It has been my experience that the offender frequently tells stories within their stories. The therapist must have the skill to see the hidden story that is being told. Shakespeare's *Hamlet,* in which a play is used to catch the king (Act II, Scene II), might provide a sophisticated example of a story within a story. The typical clinical issue is that the prisoner relates half of a story within his story. In other words, he leaves out "Chapter 1," what *he* did and focusses on "Chapter 2," what was done *to* him—in lengthy detail.

In the final chapter, I've selected what I deem to be the major issues for "Reflections and Suggestions." The reader might find little interest in one of the issues. If so, skip to the following issue that is found interesting and challenge the author.

There was one specifically unsatisfactory clinical topic—love. The reader, when the book has been read, will have noted the prisoners' responses to love on the PET, and likewise, their inability to "translate" one of Robert Frost's famous lines. The reader might be surprised by what is suggested on the last pages. Don't read it now! You have to first climb the mountain!

Chapter 2
WHAT'S IN YOUR HEART AND MIND?

As my experience extended over the years with offenders in and out of prison, I came to realize (appreciate?) their emotional life. Often group therapy at a cognitive or psychoeducational level would suddenly erupt into negative emotions. Books and numerous articles have been written focusing on the mind of the offender (criminal, prisoner). Samenow (1984), wrote a book called *Inside the Criminal Mind.* Glancing at the index, one finds these words: anger, love, murder, and violence. The concentration, however, is on the criminal's mind. The emotional aspects of crime are either totally ignored or only occasionally given a bit of consideration.

Toch (1992), a veteran and widely read concerning the life of offenders, wrote in his book *Violent Men,* "The remainder of this book reports on the results of an effort to search the minds of recurrently violent individuals" (p. 7). He did define some emotional terms: irrational violence, aggression, and violence. For example, Toch suggested, "When we talk of hostile violence-components we refer to a person's capacity for explosiveness, for reacting frustration with a stance of bitterness and hate" (p. 2). We would term these aspects disturbed emotions. The struggle for specific descriptions of the negative emotions is a difficult endeavor. Note above that Toch used bitterness, hate, and hostile. Bitterness is often associated with taste, and also includes cruelness. Hate indicates an intense aversion, or malice and odiousness, while anger suggests a strong emotion of delight, as well as the implication of a feeling of being injured or insulted.

In another book by Toch (1992), *Living in Prison,* there is mentioned, "Sometimes a frustration-aggression mechanism is at work, where the person feels retaliatory urges" (p. 57).

WORKING ALLIANCE

The following clinical method in this chapter and the other chapters assumes that the therapist (both individual and group) has established a good working alliance with the offender, especially the prisoner. A good working alliance is presently described as a give and take. It is not a mere listening, or that of a lecturer, but rather an exchange of ideas and feelings. Basically, two working agreements function: (1) they don't have to agree with me and I don't have to agree with them; (2) we *talk* out our feelings and ideas—not act them out (which brought them to prison); and (3) they can say anything they want except, "I don't know." This last stipulation is a leverage for them to think and feel either about painful dynamic material or aspects of their lives either denied, repressed, or suppressed. Of course, this stipulation applies to me! How they "love" to trap me into, "I don't know." In sum, the above has a trust theme.

The issue of a good working alliance was "established," shall we say, years ago. Before my experience of good therapy in prison, I had had years of experience in mental hospitals, alcoholic clinics, and juvenile detention centers. The prison is different. Scott (1973) wrote that when he attempted hypnosis in the first month the results were "none of the group were able to be hypnotized." However, three months later, "all the group could be relaxed (by a hypnosis method) and several of the members became good hypnotic subjects" (p. 101). This was an effective learning experience for me: timing is a critical factor in therapy.

Throughout this book, the majority of the material concerns itself with prison groups that have been functioning for some time. Specifically, a good working alliance was established with most of the group members. Some negative and hostile remarks and feelings arise (as will be noted). Typically, this negative stance is from new members in the group.

DESCRIPTIONS OF THE HEART'S FUNCTION

The title of this chapter is "What's in Your Heart and Mind?" It is difficult to separate one's heart and mind at times. Perhaps, generally, the nonprofessional notion is that heart is the center of one's emotion. These emotions can be positive: love, joy, gladness, etc.; or they can be negative: hate, lust, anger, etc. The uses of the term heart appears as a house term as illustrated in the following expressions: (1) romantic: "I love you with all my heart"; (2) verge of collapse: "My heart is broken"; (3) courage: "He has lion-hearted courage"; (4) depth of loyalty: "Deep in my heart"; (5) depression: "I'm broken hearted." The Greeks would use the phrase *dialogismoi kardion*, namely my inmost thoughts or feelings. Most Americans use "at the bottom of my heart," not "inmost heart."

Figure 1. "What's in My Heart?" A prisoner draws what's in his heart.

Enough of what others believe and teach about the heart (emotions). What do prisoners say and feel in their hearts? Three groups with whom I had a good working alliance were asked, "What's in your heart?" They were given a week to reflect, feel, recall or experience this question.

One prisoner drew the previous as a response to the question.

In all of the prisoner quotes throughout this book, names are not real. What is reported is their direct words. In a few instances, some really vulgar language has been eliminated.

The roster of prisoners used in this book covers the range of crimes: homicide, arson, sexual (rape and child molestation), armed robbery, alcohol and drug dependency, and robbery crimes. From a DSM-IV (1994) point of view, the majority had an Axis II diagnosis (paranoid, borderline, schizoid, OCPD for the most part) with Axis I sprinkled throughout (depressive, alcohol and drug dependent, ADHD, limited IQ (a few), and schizophrenia). The majority held a dual diagnosis.

GROUPS' RESPONSES

The following are three group responses to the question: "What's in your heart and mind?"

Group 1

Tom: In my heart, mistrust. I don't trust.
Pat: Loneliness and anger is in my heart. The loneliness causes the anger.
Tom: I have in my heart, fear—fear that I'd mess up again.
Joe: I have abandonment feelings in my heart and fear of facing life alone.
Ted: Pain and hurt and distrust.
Sam: Pure hatred toward myself, what I did to my victim.
Bob: I'm tired of me and of the things I do. I need a new me.
Earl: I'm better—when I came to prison I didn't care. I still get lonely, but not as bad.
Pat: Bad stuff in my heart—anger at my dad.
Jeff: Disconnected stuff—hope, frustration—and anger.

Harry:	Confused feelings and anger.
Cliff:	Anger! It gives me strength when I feel anger. It's good.
Frenchy:	I'd like to kick the world in the ass.

Group 2

Sam:	In my heart are suicidal feelings, loneliness, jealousy, and bittersweet memories. There's no life in prison.
Jeff:	Angry, lonely, lost. Feeling of being an outcast.
Tom:	Bitterness and especially depression.
Randy:	Loneliness, hurt and being timid. Fear of loosing friends in prison. My heart's on the outside, love; but in the center of my heart is emptiness and fear of death.
Sam:	Drugs, wild women and cigarettes. (The group became peeved with Sam, but he insisted on the above.)
Fred:	Depression and that I don't belong to anyone or anything. Since group therapy, there's hope that I can be what I want to be and to stop hurting people. Sam, I don't like you playing your damn game.
Randy:	Yeah. Sober up.
Sam:	I'm sorry.
Jeff:	I'd like to open up more, but I'm afraid to face myself. What others would think of me. I've been deviant all my life. (Cries)
Bo:	I'd want to kick the world in the ass. (He also added several vulgar things.)
Jake:	I'm not like Dave. I had a lot of things and didn't appreciate them.
Fred:	My heart is filled with love, anger, and loneliness.
Mike:	My heart is filled mostly with hope of getting out of prison.
Steve:	Mostly negative stuff.
Dan:	Why are we so emotionally harsh?
Steve:	People put up a wall–to survive. Can't let true feelings out. I, uh, the other night I cried.
Dave:	I'd like to behave. I'll not come back to prison. But, hell, all I know is how to manipulate.
Dr. Scott:	You manipulate me?

Dave:	I don't think I do, but if I do it, I don't know how I do it.
Ben:	Tell him the truth.
Dave:	I was in the hole for years. I developed anger.
Steve:	Who's fault? They had to control you, Dave. Don't just blame them, blame yourself.

Group 3

Ben:	I've an empty heart. I emptied it of all those things. It's cold. Every real criminal has a cold heart.
Dr. Scott:	Like a freezer?
Ben:	I can't say that. There's a little love and a little hate.
Dave:	Bitterness and coldness and a lot of hard anger.
Ben:	What does hard anger mean?
Dave:	I can't put it all together. I lash out.
Steve:	How did it get there?
Dave:	Life experiences. I was in an angry environment even in prison. And, well, I felt people were doing things to me on the streets. I began to carry a weapon.
Dr. Scott:	Less hard today?
Dave:	I'm aware of more things. Dr. Scott, you're critical. You're harsh–close to being vulgar.
Ben:	Confrontational is what he is, not harsh. I used to think he was.
Dave:	You open doors and walk in–with things that I have been struggling with all my life–hiding.
Dr. Scott:	Dave, tell the group what I've wanted you to do.
Dave:	I just can't do it. I won't. I've seen a lot of shrinks; you're different. Damn you!
Jake:	My heart is empty and angry. A lot of emptiness.
Dave:	In prison a guy can't be emotional.
Dr. Scott:	Over the years many inmates tell me that during the day "I'm a tough ass," and "At night, I sometimes cry."
Steve:	I cry in my cell, but not out of it.
Abe:	Hell, I've given up. I'd just as soon knock myself off. I cut on myself.

Glancing back at the emotions expressed by these three therapy groups of prisoners reveals a variety and in-depth emotions.

Tentatively the ensuing grouping is suggested:
1. *Empty and lonely and outcast:* this represents an existential and social aloneness. The latter suggests lack of friends; the former empty even though friends or people might be around. Perhaps lack of meaning might be a brief and somewhat accurate description.
2. *Anger, bitter, and cold:* this grouping appears to be that of the "cold," "real," or professional prisoner.
3. *Depressed, suicidal, jealous, fearful, and distrustful:* the notion of psychological/psychiatric content arises. This is the "disturbed" prisoner. When grouping 2 and 3 appear in the same prisoner, therapy has a complex and difficult though necessary undertaking.
4. *Hope and love:* although fewer than the other groupings, it did emerge. This could be called the positive emotions. It can be argued that the percentages of the various emotions expressed are not typical of all prisoners. Agreed. The sample given, however, does represent a major portion of prisoners.

At this point, no mention of the prisoner's mind has been given. There is no intention of ignoring the role of the mind and its function with prisoners thinking. Elsewhere, Scott (1971) reported a dialogue from group therapy with criminals on work release:

Paul:	The big thing about crime is the excitement, outsmarting the biggest organization in the world, the FBI, the state troopers, and the local police.
Bill:	Yeah, it's greater than sexual excitement.
Sam:	Not me, not the excitement; it's the relief of pressure. Money to feel equal.
Henry:	Money.
Fred:	I developed expensive habits.
Henry:	When I break into a home...all those presents (p. 156).

Scott (1989) wrote, "Is There a Criminal Mind?" and concluded from his experience with offenders in and out of prison that there is a criminal mind.

Scott (Palermo & Scott, 1997) was of the opinion that "the most general statement made by all offenders is, 'I'm riding a bum beef.' It is, by analogy, a kind of pledge of alliance to their 'citizenship'" (p. 97).

The present work is an effort to, finally, provide a rightful place for the emotional life of offenders—in and out of prison. We have included three papers written by prisoners regarding, "What's in my heart?"

THREE PRISONER VIGNETTES

How I Deal with Anger
Harry

Harry is a 39-year-old, divorced white male. He has three children. He is a large, six-foot, two-inch man weighing 245 pounds. He's "addicted" to exercise. He has told me several times, "Exercise helps to clear my mind. It seems to lessen my anger, for a time." Harry has been in and out of prison several times. Presently, he's in prison for attempted murder. He is a very bright man. Articulation is exellent. One goal for treatment was to have him engage his mind in positive pursuits. Harry wrote:

> As an alcoholic and heroin addict, alcohol and heroin helped to suppress the anger temporarily. I use the term temporarily because as the heroin addiction took hold the desire to quench that addiction only intensified my anger thereby releasing that anger in its irrational state by means of and through violence. While incarcerated, whenever anger arises I would use a vigorous physical workout to release and deal with anger.
>
> Today, the present, whenever anger arises I leave the situation and deal with that anger rationally and appropriately without resorting to violence.

My Anger and Me
Joe

Joe is a white male, divorced, in his late twenties. He is not large in stature, often polite, with average intelligence. This is Joe's first "visit" to prison and he trusts his last. His struggle is with himself. As you read his short description of his anger, you will note an Altered State of Consciousness (ASC). In his words, "I am a completely different person." Secondly, the psychosomatic factor, "My heartbeat . . ." In Joe's words:

> Anger and anxiety; I'm uncertain how I can put this into words, but I'll try. My thoughts of myself when angry is like I am a completely different person, until the anger is over. I do not think clearly, as I would if I weren't angry. Also my skin feels sweaty, and my heartbeat seems to pound inside my head at times.
>
> I feel very uncomfortable and get very moody, can't concentrate on things as well. Sometimes my stomach gets upset. I feel very restless and cannot relax.
>
> I need to find the ways of knowing these signs before the anger has taken over, finding ways of copying and applying methods.

Joe is, in my opinion, more of a mental health case than that of a prisoner. He was sent to prison for threatening physical harm and in his words, "losing it."

It Eats Me Up
Bob

Bob is a 29-year-old white, married male, the father of one young child. He is an emotional man, with anger and depression his most common emotion. Bob has refused medication, "I'm a man. I can work it out myself." Perhaps, his religious beliefs have, somehow, kept him from murdering. He is in prison for aggravated assault.

Bob is afraid of nothing–except himself. He has been in numerous fights; brawls might be a more accurate description. He has a broken nose and a front tooth is missing. I'm not certain about his opponent's appearance. A somewhat descriptive analogy, although out of date, is that of "Ferdinand, the Bull with the Delicate Ego." In Bob's words:

> My anger, I keep pent up. It collects. Sometimes I lose it. It comes out. I lose it and I want to kill. I get like an animal. I don't make sense.
>
> Yet, then I cry. I get on my knees in my cell and pray. My anger, my life. When I was 17 years old I threw my dad (cries) on the ground. I left home. Later, he came to me and said, "I love you." That was the most powerful moment in my life. But, uh, I had fights when I was in the service. What a struggle in me to, uh, to be kind. I blow up with rage.

This topic, as all good therapeutic topics do, provides two dynamic avenues: one to go deeper into the topic (area) or two, open up a new topic. One illustration will be given. The group focussed on a new topic the following session:

Steve: Why do people want to be hurt or cut on themselves? I don't get it.

Abe: I got to the point to where I felt I deserved it. I'd get others to do it for me–the cops or officers to beat on me. I felt I deserved it. The tension, even today, I, uh, get pissy with the guards . . .

Steve: Change, Abe, change.

Abe: I hope so.

Dave: Not me. I try to beat on the other guy first. I was in the hole five years for this. I, uh, finally got tired of it. And I'm older. After the homicide, I got angry. It's still there. Uh, the guy who pleaded. I'd not have been caught if not for that SOB.

Jake: I don't want to be on death row. It affects my sleep. I've cut my arms (shows deep cuts). I wanted to punish myself. Cut, to get the anger out of me. For years I tried to take it out on others, fights, etc. It didn't help.

Dr. Scott: Did the cutting help?

Jake: Not really. When I cut myself, it didn't hurt. But when the doc gave me a shot before sewing up the cuts–that hurt.

Steve: I'm angry, back in prison and I've wanted to take it out on others–to lash out. That's easier than taking it out on myself.

Jake: At night I cry. I'm miserable.

Dr. Scott: You've given yourself a life sentence.

Jake: Yeah, but, I can't . . . (silence).

Steve: Get it out–talk about it.

Jake: I yelled and screamed.

Dave: Hacking on yourself doesn't help.

Steve: Can't you accept death?

Jake: I'm fearful. I can't accept death.

Steve: Religion helps.

Abe: It eats at me. That's where I'm stuck. I'd rather kill myself. But I have a yellow streak up my back , so I'll get the officers to do it.

Attending to the last prisoner's stated experience of his dilemma, "It eats at me," we wonder if this is a type of "prisoner-cancer." "It eats at me," yet Abe seemingly will not kill himself but will attempt to get the officers to do it for him. When out of prison, the potential for provoking someone to violently attack him is most probable. Several authors have written concerning the self-injuring phenomenon. Favazza and Simeon (1994) have described three types of self-injuring phenomenon: (1) major: frequently this occurs with individuals who have a psychotic condition; (2) stereotypical: this is a repetitive type, but lacks associated content; and (3) superficial: no intent of serious (deadly) effects.

In my opinion, Abe has a borderline personality disorder. Typically, studies have found this personality disorder to be associated with the self-injuring phenomenon. Although often considered to be not classed as serious, Abe has the probability. Jake is clearly a serious case. He is psychotic and hallucinates regularly concerning his victims. His wounds were not superficial.

THE PRISONER AND THE WORLD

The majority of this group of prisoners indicated coldness and anger. A clinical approach of using Frost was considered. Frost (1971) had written an epitaph. The last sentence was: "I had a lover's quarrel with the world" (p. 14). Untermeyer has reflected on Frost's epitaph and suggested that a person can question the world, "but always with understanding, always with earnest love" (p. 14). Frost's epitaph and Untermeyer's reflection were read to the three groups who had responded to "What's in your heart and mind?" They were asked to indicate their feelings and thoughts concerning the world. Frenchy's statement was quoted (from Group 1), "I'd like to kick the world in the ass."

Group 1

Red: The world sucks. Damn it, no one to blame. I hate prison. Yet, I'd rather be here than out there. At first I wanted capital punishment. Suicide? I'd rather not plan it, just let it pop up when I'm down.

Frenchy: I don't give a damn about the world, and I'm mad at this prison.

Mike: I don't like the world or anything in it.

Yoki: I like prison a lot better than the world. The government is all messed up.

Kevin: I came to prison in my teens. I really don't know the world. I've tried to make the prison a place in which to grow.

Ted: I hate prison. I screwed up in the world. Therapy is scary, facing myself.

Group 2

Andy: I was married. I had a quarrel with my wife. I left home. Then, uh, the murder. At first I made prison romantic. Then it got real and I got in fights. I got to blaming everyone but myself. Finally, in group therapy I'm facing myself.

Tony: In prison I hate the staff and inmates. With the world, I was depressed and confused.

Larry: Fuck the world. I hate everything.

Ed: Prison was a life saver for me. I'd been killed or I'd have killed someone.

Bob: I've quarreled a lot, but it's a quarrel with myself.

Group 3

Ted: The world is miserable. Too much hatred and politics. (You hate?) Yeah, kinda. I was raising shit (new member to group).

Steve: I hate what's in the world. Wars and hate most of the people–they're phony.

Dr. Scott: How about drug dealers?
Steve: I hate drug dealers and I was one of 'em. It ruins life, kills people. I have a daughter—I have to stay out of prison for her.
Dave: I hate people.
Dr. Scott: Hate me?
Dave: You brought out the shit in me—you're a shit stirrer.
Dr. Scott: That's a good epitaph!
Bill: You have to get yourself out.
Tom: Well, I was in a fight and I killed the guy. I felt a surge. I went too far.
Sam: I hate everything about prison—nothing is productive.
Dr. Scott: Hate group therapy?
Tom: No, it's a step.
Bob: I used to love nature...but I got on drugs. In prison all one learns is to be a better convict.
Ted: Bob, you're right. I've learned slick ways to break into a house. Cut the main cord and the alarm system won't go off.
Sam: Easy to live in prison, good food. The real world is tough. I've been locked up most of my life.
Mickey: I don't hate the world. I hate prison.

The majority of these prisoners indicate that they hated or were angry at the world. A very few expressed a "lover's quarrel," where there is concern and love. Perhaps the conclusion is too broad, with "holes" of escape, but the majority failed to have a "lover's quarrel" (as suggested by Frost's idea) with anyone or anything or the world.

These prisoners were read a newspaper article entitled: "New Health Villains: Anger, Anxiety" (Talan, 1996). In brief, the article reported data from various labs indicating that mental stress, especially anger and anxiety, are more likely to provoke a heart attack than other factors: diet, lack of exercise, and genetics.

If these prisoners can't have a "lover's quarrel" with the world, perhaps they can have "a lover's scare" concerning their health.

Post (1992) has provided a summary for much of this chapter. He wrote that psychosocial stressors may become encoded at a physiological level. In turn, "minor stressors or losses may come to play a role in the triggering of affective episodes" (p. 1004).

Chapter 3

THE BRAIN AND LOVE?

The term love is often misused, even abused. Frequently love is used in a trifling sense. Car bumper stickers read: I (heart sign) my dog. The prize goes to the bumper sticker: I (heart sign) what's-his-name.

Psychiatry and psychology textbooks, for the most part, write sparingly (if at all) about love. This is not merely our opinion. Maslow (1970) wrote years ago, "It is amazing how little empirical sciences have to offer on the subject of love" (p. 81). In sharp contrast, psychiatry and psychology texts allow ample space for sex. DSM-IV (1994) has several diagnoses for sexual problems; for instance, Male Hypoactive Sexual Desire, Female Sexual Arousal Disorder, etc. Apparently the topic of love is left for talk shows, self-help books, and daily newspaper "counselors."

Freud wrote extensively, almost exhaustingly, concerning sexual matters as readers of this book know. It might, however, come as a bit of a surprise that Freud (1959) also wrote, "In the development of mankind as a whole, just as in individuals, love alone acts as the civilizing factor in the sense that it brings a change from egoism to altruism" (p. 35).

Other outstanding authors, especially two psychologists (Erikson and Maslow) have offered their ideas and descriptions of love. Erikson (1964) described love as a "mutuality of devotion forever subduing the antagonisms inherent in divided function" (p. 129). We assume that implies passing over–maturing out–of egoism to altruism, as previously suggested by Freud.

Maslow (1970) devoted an entire chapter, "Love In Self-Actualizing People." Our judgement is that Maslow's ideas are excellent. Among the characteristics Maslow indicated was "The Ability to Love and to be Loved," and "Dropping of Defenses." If this work is unknown for the reader, it would be advantageous to secure it, or a comparable one.

EROS VS. AGAPE

Distinctions of eros and agape are appropriate. The latter is love which is giving; the former is love as taking. In mature love, both of these variables are present. In love which lacks maturity, love can be entirely associated with eros, or merely sex. Philia (Greek for brotherly) indicates a love of friendship. As might be expected, there was a Greek god of love. He was Eros. He was a creative god, doing all types of attractive and good things. Greek mythology regressed. In later Greek mythology, Eros was associated with lust. There was also a Greek goddess of love–Aphrodite. She performed all types of love variables, among her duties was that of inspiring affection. She herself was a most gorgeous beauty, perhaps, equivalent to a Miss America. To increase her attractiveness, as though that were needed, she wore a girdle which had magical powers. By comparisons, Miss America wears a swimsuit. Aphrodite had many affairs. It seems that the majority of prisoners believe (needed to believe?) that all women wear magical girdles. This, they felt, could not be resisted, for which they were thankful!

Dunne (1978) has made the distinction between mind and heart, wherein the former is to know, while the latter is to be known. This distinction has an appeal. Clinically, many wives have said, "My husband doesn't really know me, and he seems to have little interest in knowing me. We lack intimacy in our marriage. I yearn to be known by him."

KARDIA AND ITS VARIOUS MEANINGS

In the previous chapter, we attempted to describe heart as suggestive of emotions, feelings, etc. Palermo (1994) has proposed a description of emotions when he wrote, "An emotion is a feeling state, a feeling tone, present in an individual at a certain time." He further noted that other authors relate emotions "as an augmentation beyond a certain level of a feeling that may be joy, sadness" (p. 43). A bit of history of *kardia* (heart) has had several meanings. *Kardia* has implied a place where moral decisions are made, what we today call conscience. Or *kardia* has been the equivalent of the mind. In the Bible (1966) (Old Testament), to know a person's heart is to know his thoughts. Finally, *kardia,* as previously mentioned, implies emotions, affections, impulses, feelings, etc. In this sense, to "keep someone in your heart" involves a fondness, an affection; whereas, to know someone in one's mind is to have intellectual knowledge.

Gabbard (1992) has pointed an index finger at the necessity for non-biological variables. He wrote, "To lose the psychodynamic perspective is to lose the complexity and richness of human functioning in the quicksand of neurotransmitters and molecular genetics. To our great good fortune, mind and brain are inseparable" (p. 997). The present effort is to gather all the variables together. Under this umbrella we have to gather a well-rounded view of prisoners–their brain, heart, and love. Should evil be included? Slovenko (1995) reported that among the numerous ideas suggested for entries in DSM-IV (1994), "evil was not among them" (p. 296).

During one group therapy session with prisoners, three members of the group had committed homicide; all three of them had more than one homicide.

Steve: I tried to feel bad about my victim. But it backfired. In my dream they killed me.
George: That's normal. All who have killed have dreamt that the victim tries to kill and does. That happened to me.
Dr. Scott: George, I'll show you that you're wrong.
George: No you won't.
Dr. Scott: George, ask Gus.
George: Gus, you've murdered. Have you dreamt of your victim killing you?
Gus: Not at all.
George: Damn it, Gus. You are different.
Steve: In my first dream, I dreamt my victims that I killed were getting out of their graves to music. They got me.
Dr. Scott: For you two, Steve and George, a corpse is not dead.
Steve: Yeah.
George: And how!

The above material regarding Steve and George, as well as other prisoner feelings and thoughts, prompted an article (Scott, 1996), "When Isn't a Corpse Dead?" What of Gus? Gus was what might be called "a card-carrying paranoid." In his firm belief, he had to murder before he was murdered. Hence, he justified his actions. Nothing in the trial emerged to indicate that his beliefs were accurate.

Returning to Steve, he was questioned, "Remember, Steve, that last week you said you killed a cat and were upset. It seems that you were more upset with that than your homicides."

Steve: I've never thought of it that way.
Dr. Scott: Think about it now.
Steve: I can see the cat's face, terrible. I look at the guy I killed and I say too fucking bad.
Gus: Hatred is strength. Something to live for. I think of suicide everyday; hate pulls me out.
Steve: What I've not faced is that I'll never get out of this f—- prison.

In this brief excerpt from group, we have captured a window of hate and justification—shall we say evil? Gus loves hate. It keeps him from suicide. Steve's pathological judgement has him value a cat's life over a human being's. Steve only "sobers up" when he looks at his position—in prison for life. He's not faced that, in spite of living with it for years. A touch of reality enters, even with this hardened "psychopathic-narcissist" when he looks at himself for a moment.

BIOLOGICAL VS. SOCIAL ASPECTS OF THE BRAIN

We now turn to the important topic of the brain. Just how is it constructed and what are a few of its parts?

Kemker (1995) began her remarks by quoting from Guze's (1989) speech, "Biological Psychiatry: Is There Any Other Kind?" From Guze's speech, Kemker selected, "I believe that continuing debate about the biological basis of psychiatry is derived much more from philosophical, ideological, and political concerns than from scientific ones" (p. 322). Kemker chose three areas from scientific (biological) psychiatry that "are fraught with 'metameaning' and buried assumptions" (p. 245). For her argument, Kemker selected:

1. *Genetic loading:* In essence, regarding family "is a statement of correlation–the presence of some shared genes and the presence of shared mental illness" (p. 245). As the reader knows, correlation doesn't indicate causality. Kemker pointed to this significant distinction.
2. *Chemical imbalance:* In training Kemker was taught (as a resident) that mental illness is similar to diabetes which is "a chemical imbalance in the body." So also is mental illness.
3. *Noncompliance:* The patient doesn't follow what he was told–to take meds.

A well-respected psychiatrist, Eisenberg, also selected Guze as a worthy opponent regarding the brain's biology. Eisenberg (1995) penned a timely and thought-provoking article. His first sentence was, "The central proposition of this article is that the human brain is constructed socially" (p. 1563). In an effort to establish his argument, Eisenberg pointed to the changes made in DSM-IV (1994). Specifically, he pointed out that a variety of disorders "not quite 30 years later, all four disorders (schizophrenia, depression, obsessive-compulsion and alzheimers) reveal a subtle interpenetration of psychosocial and biological factors in their pathogenesis" (p. 1569).

Eisenberg concluded his ideas by replying to Guze who had previously given a lecture entitled, "Biological Psychiatry: Is There Any Other?" Countering Guze, Eisenberg wrote, "Social Psychiatry: Is There Any Other Kind?" (p. 1571). Perhaps, in the present instance we can state, "A Brain With Love and Hate: Is There Any Other Kind?" A reader might question my assumptions as philosophical ones–a regression of a clinical psychologist turned philosopher.

What does research offer? Andreasen (1984), a physician, has indicated, "It (the brain) is the source of our ability to speak, to laugh, to write, to think, to create, to love, to despair, and to hate" (p. 83). We note that love and hate are included as abilities of the brain according to Andreasen, a physician. Hence, a more appropriate title for this present chapter would be: "The Brain: Love, Hate and _____ Within."

What word belongs in that blank space? Evil? Despair? Hope? All of these terms? Below are the words of one prisoner (Charlie) as he struggles to examine what's in his mind, heart (emotions) and beliefs. As Gabbard (1992) has argued, this prisoner has not lost himself "in the quicksand of neurotransmitter or molecular genetics" (p. 997).

PRISONER VIGNETTE: WHAT'S AT THE BOTTOM OF MY HEART

Charlie

Originally in group I said that despair was deep in my heart. But after some thought, I think this might not be all, because I am inclined to think I would already be dead if this were the case.

I have some hope also that will last me for a time, but I don't feel hope runs eternal. It has its limits and I've gotten to where I can now see the limits. It is at times that I ask my self how much more, and why do I hate myself so much. Yes, that's there too. Often I submerse my feelings in day-to-day distractions, but when the world presses too tight, at times my emotions come out. Like I have nothing to lose. Then I think of what a loser I am and all the other negative self talk.

But deeper than all this I think and hope perhaps there is peace. And I think deep down that I am a good person. Or as I heard somewhere, a good person with bad ideas. Somewhere I think my heart is in the right place, but I feel overwhelmed with so much trash. I can't let it feel because if I open my heart, it'll be crushed by my own making. Maybe that is all self-centered. I'm not sure. I do care about all who I've wronged and actually believe I loved them. And I believe there is peace to be had in the future. I have made a commitment to myself not to victimize anyone in any way. Maybe therein lies peace. In the bottom of my heart, there may be love.

The unity of personhood gains further evidence by the article, "Mind, Body, Immune System," by Carpenter and Strauss (1992). They stated, "It is well known that the immune system has memory cells–specialized lymphocytes (a type of white blood cell) that are produced to fight an infection" (p. 2). Further on they pointed out that "The CNS, the endocrine system, and the immune system all participate in the response to transient, repeated, and chronic psychological stress" (p. 2). Among the psychological stresses were job loss, divorce, depression, and anxiety. We would add that, for some prisoners, living in prison is a chronic psychological stress.

The following note is by a prisoner struggling with a variety of emotions. He contrasts the structure of prison and its variables against treatment programs:

> Doctor Scott,
>
> I really think the isolation, combined with the constant cruelty that we are faced with daily, is a really easy factor to abuse other emotions, such as anger. I don't think love has a chance to be felt in our environment. I've felt a couple of infatuations, but they were fleeting. The structure of prison environment plus a whole load of treatment and programs tend to wean us off of the love we thought we never got, whether erroneous or not.

It would appear, at least for this prisoner, that his CNS, endocrine, and immune system are losing the struggle with his experienced chronic psychological stress. The authors (Carpenter & Strauss, 1992) suggested a number of activities: exercise, relaxation, writing, etc. In their article, they did not have prisoners in mind. The quoted prisoner above added this note two weeks later:

> I have kept some civilization with me; my radio for music and most of all news; a newspaper for on the record news, local and regional and world news; magazines for world news. Many, many memories of camping in the mountains, on the coast hunting clams, catching crabs, boating in a boat club that my family were members of. So, I'm still hanging in there when it comes to keeping up with the daily news and keeping abreast of even the styles of cars that are out there in civilization right now.

His efforts suggest a method of "escaping" the prison by what's happening in "civilization" (his term) by means of news. In addition, he uses happy memories of the past: camping, boating, and family. In my judgement, he is employing Pruyser's (1983) "tutored fantasy." Tutored fantasy comes under the general heading of Illusionistic World. Pruyser was specific and forceful in this matter. He wrote, "By this placement I wish to correct in some measure the idea, dominant in much of the psychoanalytic literature, that the autistic and the realistic worlds are the only two worth considering" (p. 65). Tutored fantasies are described by Pruyser as "orderly imagination that has produced novels, poetry, theological and philosophical propositions, musical compositions, choreographic works, and scientific models"

(p. 66). In Chapter 6, the reader will encounter tutored fantasy as they read created fairy tales by prisoners. One of the fairy tales will be written by the above noted prisoner named Bill.

EVIL

Earlier in this chapter, reference was made regarding Slovenko's (1995) point that evil was not accepted for inclusion in DSM-IV. How different in England. *The British Journal of Psychiatry* **requested** (my emphasis) an article on evil from Professor Prins. He entitled his article "Psychiatry and the Concept of Evil," with a subtitle, "Sick in Heart or Sick in Mind?" (1994). Prins' article, in fact it was a guest article, briefly summarizes various opinions from a variety of authors. He considered that "evil is being equated somewhat arbitrarily with serious criminal wrong-doing, notably that involving the infliction of persistent, gratuitous personal violence" (p. 298).

In my opinion, an excellent book is that of Ellenberger (1970). It affords a rather good historical view of this interesting and complex issue. Ellenberger wrote, "The emergence of dynamic psychiatry can be traced to the year 1775, to a clash between the physician Mesmer and the exorcist Gassner" (p. 53). Briefly, Mesmer, the founder of hypnosis, insisted that people became better (cured?) by his hypnosis due to animal magnetism in his (Mesmer's) body. Whereas, Gassner, a Catholic priest, claimed that his subjects became better due to exorcism, that is, driving out the devil. Mesmer's "new ideas" prevailed. The topic of evil, the devil, and the supernatural appear in several pages of this well-accepted text.

The interested reader will further his/her knowledge of this topic by reading Meissner's (1992) book, *Ignatius of Loyola*. Meissner is a Catholic priest and also a psychoanalyst. In the preface, Meissner wrote, "It brings into focus significant questions about the complex interplay between human motivation and needs on one side and religious experience and spiritual motivation on the other" (p. ix). In his attempt to present clearly the intriguing question noted above, Meissner utilized Arieti's (1967) notions regarding the difference between psychotic and religious mystical states.

Potentially helpful in this presentation would be terms which are in sharp contrast to evil. Some of these words are:

1. *Eutopelia* means a happy (or merry) wisdom. This stands in sharp contrast to phthanos which indicates an attraction, even a dislike for the good. In Greek *eu* is the word for good or well. Examples are: euphoney and eulogy.
2. *Eumenides* (etymology: *eu* = good plus *manos* = mind) means gracious people.
3. *Eudaimonism* means happiness, and *eudaimonia* means ability to produce happiness.

One might grasp a fuller understanding by introducing the concept of Altered State of Consciousness (ASC). An ASC implies that as a result of an activity (physical or mental) the individual's typical level of experience is changed. Drugs are the easy avenue to an ASC. But physical activity, running or jogging, often results in a change of experience most likely due in part to an alteration of endorphins. Music changes one's mood and hence feelings. What is presently proposed is that evil–the evil activity–produces an ASC. In brief, the evil activity produces a "high."

ALTERED STATE OF CONSCIOUSNESS: A NEW ENTRY–EVIL

Ludwig (1966), in his seminal and well accepted article on ASC, listed the adaptive and maladaptive experiences associated with an ASC. He listed eight maladaptive uses. Delight (or a "high") in evil activity was not in that list. I want to add to Ludwig's list of maladaptive experiences–evil.

At this point, statements made by prisoners might further this topic.

Ted: I get so angry I want to kill.
Ben: I thought I had a demon. I was lonely and depressed and not in my right mind.
Dr. Scott: If a person doesn't believe in demons, how can he be possessed? Some of you fellows have just said that you didn't believe in demons.
Ben: Demons pick on weak people.

Ted: I believe in evil. Look at Hitler and Bundy, and the dying in Africa—those two tribes slaughtering one another.

Dave: People can be possessed by evil. I know I was.

Joe: People create their own evil. Good God, three in this group said they'd kill their own father.

Ben: Yeah, but I can't believe it. My dad loved me.

Ted: Some dads have done some terrible stuff.

Later, further remarks by prisoners will be given. Perhaps the title of this chapter should have been: "The Brain: Love, Hate and Evil."

And therapy? A most brief response to this challenging question is: *metanoia*. *Metanoia* is from the Greek: *met* = to cross over; *noein* = to think. Hence, etymologically *metanonia* means changing one's mind. In clinical practice it implies to change one's life style or to "turn around."

We will offer one example: Ben (called Big Ben) stated: "I've a history of anger. When frustrated, I get angry. But after treatment, I have some control. Say, oh, well, six or eight months ago I saw red. That's all I could see. But, I didn't go back to my old convict life. Even in prison there's something to lose. Well, after seeing the red, I stopped and thought..."; he stopped for a few moments then added, "We have to either go to seed or continue to grow. By going to seed, I mean reached your level."

In the last chapter, I will provide an extended discussion of evil, as well as make suggestions regarding love.

Chapter 4

PRISONERS' EXPRESSION TEST (PET)

The author, being a psychologist, must choose wisely from a plethora of psychological instruments. Overuse of testing needs to be avoided, as well as a reaction formation against the use of psychological testing. My experience indicates that psychiatrists follow one of two routes: they use the MMPI and have it scored or use clinical psychologists. Regarding social workers and their use of psychological testing, I have no clear impression.

Van Voorhis (1994), in her book *Psychological Classification of Adult Prison Inmates*, has summarized the major classification for prisoners by means of psychological testing. Her grouping centers around: (1) the MMPI and Megaree's research; (2) Interpersonal Maturity Level (I-level); (3) Quay's Adult Internal Management Systems (AIMS); (4) the Jesness Inventory; and (5) Conceptual Level. Van Voorhis concluded her book with the following opinion: "The singularly most important observation made throughout the preceding four chapters: there are compelling psychological differences among inmates with regard to their experiences of the prison environment" (p. 261). This conclusion has been clearly evident from a clinical experience. In previous publications, we have reported on a variety of different groups in prison (Scott, 1993; and Palermo and Scott, 1997).

Another orientation is that of Walters, who through a series of publications has worked on the thinking styles of criminals. Recently, Walters (1996) has published an article entitled "The Psychological Inventory of Criminal Thinking Styles: Part III Predictive Validity." In general, his instrument had predictive value even independent of the age (youth) variable.

Toch (1992), a well-recognized author in the arena of prisons, has published the PPI (Prison Preference Inventory) in his book *Living in Prison*. It is an inventory focussed on assessing the prisoners' response to his environment, the prison. Among the numerous reasons for using the PPI, Toch stated, "An instrument of this kind isolates possible problem people tentatively but quickly and allows us to allocate limited resources to them" (p. 378).

CONSTRUCTION OF THE PET

For a period of time, I used the PPI in my prison work. It was useful in indicating some issues with the prisoners but, in my opinion, lacked depth. For a period of time, I experimented with a psychological instrument named PET (Prisoners Expression Test). Scott first introduced the PET to the professional literature in Palermo and Scott (1997). Ten years prior, with private patients, he had gradually developed a test, which appears to have been quite helpful in assessing a variety of patient problems. For the prisoners some items were added, for instance: Prison life_____; Criminals_____; etc.

The reader can turn to Appendix I at the end of this chapter for illustrations of the PET. It has 53 questions which require responses. In format, it has the sentence completion test structure. Two features have been added: (1) instructions: "Take your time. Answer as accurately as possible;" and (2) featured as a well-rounded clinical assessment: inter- and extra-personal, memory, present time, and the future. The two samples in the Appendix are not extreme samples but tend to be in the average grouping.

Regarding the present sample, it reflects a brief span in which prisoners attending my group therapy sessions were asked to complete the PET. The sample of thirty-three is small, but it is my judgement that it is reflective of numerous prisoners. In the process five tests had to be eliminated due to partial completion or mental confusion. One OCPD prisoner worked hours to complete the PET.

RESEARCH RESULTS OF THE PET

For the present purpose, we have selected several "key" questions, tabbed the responses, and given actual responses from the PET. Brief academic and/or clinical ideas are tendered. An attempt has been made to group questions as suggested below.

Questions   **Typical Expressions**

A. Prison Life
   I. Prison life (question 1)
      A. Good (ok) = 13   ("not much different than on the streets")
      B. Bad (poor) = 15   ("caged up like a wild animal")
      C. Uncertain = 5
   2. Criminals (question 22)   No clear responses emerged, but covered a wide range: "We are the scum of the earth" to "Criminals are from every walk of life."

   3. Laws in this country (question 24)
      A. Unjust (bad) = 16   ("laws stink")
      B. Fair (good) = 13   ("are for the benefit of people to get along and to prevent serious tragedies")

Comment: Overall, there tends to be a division regarding prison life and laws. Hence, generalization requires caution on these two points.

B. Family Life
   1. My childhood (question 2)
      A. Good (ok) = 9   ("generally a positive experience")
      B. Poor (terrible) = 24   ("my childhood was fucked")
   2. My mother (question 25)
      A. Good = 18   ("is a very nice person")
      B. Bad (cruel) = 12   ("left us when we were young")
   3. My father (question 28)
      A. Good (ok) = 10   ("was a good person")
      B. Bad (cruel) = 14   ("is a piece of shit")
      C. Not in the home = 9

Both of the quotes above regarding parents are from two prisoners (questions 25 and 28), clearly an indication of one good and one bad parent.

Comment: Of all the 53 questions, the question concerning childhood (question 2) is the most skewed in the negative direction. We need to question the response score. How accurate are the answers? It is a learned response from TV and "pop psychology" which appears to suggest that most of us come from dysfunctional families. Is it taught in prison by those prisoners that look at others for their problems?

Moreover, there were 18 good mothers and 10 good fathers. Could it be that the dominant parent set the tone for the family? Scott (1989) conducted a study of nonalcoholic adult children from alcoholic homes. Among the interesting findings were those regarding: "The dominant parent–is he or she the psychiatrically sick one, or the normal one?" (p. 70). Scott noted that a female respondent wrote, "Mother was the most difficult. She was always upset–mad all the time" (p. 70). The father was alcoholic but not the dominant parent. To further this important but complex problem, Bowlby (1988) has argued (we believe successfully) concerning the Freudian view who stressed the mind, and that of Meyer who favored real factors and events. Bowlby stressed that, "The central task of developmental psychiatry is to study the endless interactions of the internal and the external" (p. 1). It is our hypothesis that the current study points to this complex issue regarding the childhood life of future prisoners.

C. Love
1. I love (question 7)
   A. Myself = 8   ("myself")
   B. No one = 9   ("no one")
   C. My children = 5   ("my little baby")
   D. God = 3   ("God")
   E. Mother = 2   ("my mother a lot")
   F. Father = 2   ("my dad")
   G. Etc. = 4   ("I love sex and whiskey")
2. The person who most loves me (question 47)
   A. Don't know = 8   ("really don't know")
   B. Mother = 7   ("my mom")
   C. Father = 4   ("Dad has always...")
   D. Myself = 3   ("myself and I")
   E. Girlfriend = 3   ("she's out there waiting")
   F. A scattering of selections ("grandmother, children," etc)
3. The person I most love (question 36)

This question is a "close-copy" of question 7, which leaves a wide range of responses. Question 36 points to a person. In fact, there were no major (significant) differences in replies.

Comment: Love is a much overused and misused word. In Chapter 3, we were specific, using descriptions from Maslow (1970) and Erikson (1964), as well as others. What seems to emerge, especially from question 47, is that of primary narcissism, in which love is either directed toward the self or to no one else. The process, really a struggle, to mature from self love to love of another is a long and bumpy road. Hence, short courses, or psychoeducation courses, appear in our judgement to be superficial and unproductive.

In about half of the respondents, love of family (mother, father or children) did emerge. How deep and how effective is the realistic and different question.

Samenow (1984) has taken the position that criminals have their "deepest sentimentality" for their mothers (p. 166). The present data, we believe, indicates a wide range from love to rejection. One of my patient prisoners expressed himself regarding his mother by writing, "Some women should never be allowed to have kids or raise them. It would stop a lot of the problems in crime." This hardly reflects Samenow's sentimental idea regarding mothers. The above response was not unique. Another prisoner wrote, "My mother was too busy with drugs or alcohol to care for me." And again, "My mother instead of admitting mistakes is still in severe denial about anything she may have done wrong."

In short, generalizations concerning mothers by prisoners require the factor of providing an opportunity to have the prisoner respond freely, not in a context which seemingly provides a provoked response.

D. Existential Group
  1. God (question 15)
     A. Real (and personal) = 19   ("is my love")
     B. No God = 8   ("is not")
     C. Don't know = 6   ("a confusing idea")
  2. Death (question 16)
     A. The end = 14   ("is forthcoming and natural")
     B. Welcome it = 12   ("Yes, please!")
     C. Fear it = 7   ("I'm afraid")

Comment: It was a surprise (for me) to learn how many of the subjects of this group welcome death. As a result, I'm uncertain how this finding can be generalized. One tentative correlation from this group is: if God is real and personal, death should not be a feared event. In general, there was a correlation. Yet, other associations are not so clear. An example is "God is too busy to worry about my problems" and "Death doesn't really scare me; it's the unknown after life that does." Another prisoner wrote suggesting a type of ambivalence both regarding God and death. Finally, one prisoner wrote, "I don't believe in God" and "I don't like death. It's no good." This prisoner has two homicide convictions.

We neither fostered nor shunned religious or spiritual discussions. At times, a lively–perhaps heated–disagreement arose between religious-oriented prisoners and prisoner atheists. This was used to further two basic goals: (1) TALK it out, don't ACT it out; and (2) we can disagree and still be friends. For people unaware of prison life, the above-named goals represent hurdles–major ones. Generally, not only for this arena, but in other areas, progress was made.

E. Victimization
   1. I feel a victim of (question 8)
      A. Others = 21   ("my father was always after me")
      B. Myself = 10   ("my own evil")
      C. Everything = 1
      D. Nothing = 1
   2. Behind my back people say (question 10)
      A. Negative things = 26   ("He's a geek, a freak")
      B. Good things = 4   ("good things about me")
      C. Don't care = 3   ("Who cares; I can't control that")

Comment: These two questions focus on what others do or say about an individual. It is not an objective question in that it "invites" a negative response. However, previous research (Palermo & Scott, 1997) has rather definitely indicated a victimization/paranoid orientation of prisoners. What needs to be done is to compare a normal group of individuals with a prison group regarding questions 8 and 10.

Given the above considerations, question 10 has the greatest difference of all the 53 questions: 26 negative responses to 4 good responses. Three respondents indicated they didn't care. Comparing question 10 to question 8, the general trend (being a victim) continues. Yet,

10 prisoners did note that they are a victim of their "own stuff"–thoughts, actions, beliefs, or feelings. These 10 prisoners I know rather well. They have made significant therapeutic advances.

  F. Self-reflecting Questions
    1. If I could change one thing about me (question 12)
       There were no clear trends. Some examples are: my race, my temper, my penis size, my mind (twice), my weight (twice), thinking of my crime (a brutal murder), etc.
    2. I'm most guilty about (question 20)
       A. My crime = 6   ("my crimes")
       B. Not guilty = 9   ("I am not")
       C. Hurting others = 5   ("beating my father")
       D. My temper = 3   ("when I lose my temper and what I then do")

Comment: This is, in my opinion, a good response for over half of the responders: 24 of 33 prisoners have the maturity to shoulder responsibility for their behavior. These prisoners indicate a willingness to look at themselves, in brief, to put themselves under observation. What of the others? We can be specific with one prisoner. On his first PET, he wrote, "I am not guilty." At a later testing, to the same question, he wrote, "I'm guilty for what I did–my crime."

A shortcoming of the present work is that a formal follow-up of the PET was not done. As is so often in actual clinical work, the clinician hasn't the resources to do research associated with his/her clinical tasks.

  G. Sexual and Obsessional Thoughts of Sex and Other Things
    1. My sexual life (question 9)
       Note: The question was poorly asked; it should have been a two-part question: presently and before prison. Some respondents answered this question as applied to the present, others to life before prison.
       A. Present time
          1. Masturbate = 15   ("I masturbate")
          2. Nonexistent = 5   ("no sex life")
       B. Before prison
          1. Good = 6   ("always filled with lots of fun and excitement")

    2. Not good = 7   ("was and is dysfunctional. To this day in order to ejaculate, I need fantasy of ——" (female family members))
  2. I can't stop thinking of (question 38)
    A. Sex = 10   ("having a sexual relation with ex-mother-in-law")
    B. Guilt = 5   ("my murdered victim")
    C. Life out of prison = 5 ("the future, out of prison")
    D. The person who turned me in = 5 ("why —— told the cops")
    E. My no good attorney = 4 ("killing my attorney")
    F. Death = 3   ("of death–fear")
    G. God = 1   ("of God")

Comment: The grouping of sexual and "can't stop thinking of" are in many ways not associated. Yet for nearly a third of the respondents it is associated. The issue of sex will be further considered. Chapter 8, "For Prisoners: Sex in the Key of C," will attempt to explore this difficult issue.

For another subgroup of respondents to question 38, there is a profound separation between guilt (remorse) versus a paranoid angry stance. *Once again, we learn and must keep the lessons in mind–how diverse these groups of prisoners really are.*

Regarding the sexual issue with prisoners, it does appear, for some, that it is a "phallic fixation." Sandler and A. Freud (1985) discuss "love fixation." A. Freud, in describing fixation wrote that, "It always means an undue amount of libido has been left behind" (p. 198). This means that an individual continues to make something important from an earlier phase of development. Bettelheim (1976) is convinced that the fairy tale *Jack and the Beanstalk* is a phallic tale. He wrote, "Getting stuck in the phallic phase is little progress over fixation on the oral phase" (p. 190). My clinical experience suggests, for some, a phallic fixation. Furthermore, it has occurred to me that some prisoners have "crime fixation"–it brings excitement, getting away with things and putting it over on adults. *A major task of therapy is to break the "crime fixation" and the "phallic fixation."*

  H. Tell All; Tell Nothing
    The format for this group will be changed. Question 42 is "What I don't want to tell you," while question 43 is "What I most want to tell

you." For all 33 respondents their replies will be given "matched" so-to-speak.

Question 42 **What I don't want to tell you**	Question 43 **What I most want to tell you**
1. I can't make decisions	I want to prove that I can do it
2. I'm afraid	I'm trying
3. I cross dress	Others know what is best for me
4. Nothing	I'm not sick
5. I'm bothered day and night	It's hard to hide from you
6. The truth of my world	I can be ok
7. Who I am	God is love
8. What I really think of myself	How I think
9. I cry at night, often	Ready for parole
10. I'm truly lost	I need help
11. I wrote something for you	Don't give up on me
12. I was an offender early in life	This group has helped me a lot
13. I don't know	I need help
14. My sex thoughts–embarrassed	About my discoveries
15. About my crime	I want help
16. I'm afraid you'd use it against me	I'm a coward
17. Nothing	About my family
18. Who I am	I can't do it
19. I wouldn't tell anyone	About God
20. Depression – really down	I'm a coward who preys on kids
21. I don't trust anyone	You need to believe me
22. My bad stuff	My fears
23. I won't tell you	I'm living in hell
24. Too personal	I need help
25. My sexual fantasies	I don't like your style of therapy
26. Everything–I need help	Everything
27. I'm like my mother so much, I hate myself	Thank you
28. Fear when I'm out of prison	I feel like a lost puppy
29. Fearful that I'm a lost cause	Sex can't be for me
30. I need to be believed	I went two years to college
31. I won't	Please, help me
32. Not important to me or you	Good grasp of the future
33. Can't make decisions	I'm a good man

Comment: The vast majority of the responses were accurate. Only three responses to question 42 (What I don't want to tell you) tended to be "smart ass" (4, 7, and 31) with tell you "nothing." Perhaps the majority of responses could be grouped under "Who I am," is what I don't want to tell you. Examples are "I cross dress," "I cry at night," "I'm lost," and "My sexual fantasies." Whereas, the trends to question 43 (what I most want to tell you) were that of needing help or "I'm trying," "Don't give up on me," and "I'm a coward." The responses to both questions (42 and 43) have been most useful for discussion topics during group therapy sessions. Names are not used, but areas have been mentioned. Most often this does lead to disclosure by the prisoner, which in turn always (well, nearly always) promotes other in-depth self disclosures.

I. Self-Reflecting Group
   1. What I don't understand about me (question 29)
      A. Can't be what I want to be = 18 ("why I am what I am")
      B. My behavior = 8 ("my self-defeating behavior")
      C. My alcohol and drug abuse = 4 ("why I keep doing drugs")
      D. Why I hate myself = 3 ("why I hate myself so much")
   2. My problem is (question 49)
      A. Paranoid = 6 ("I trust no one")
      B. Myself = 5 ("I'm weird")
      C. Sex = 5 ("I can't get enough sex")
      D. My mind = 5 ("dealing with my thoughts")
      E. Anger (rage) = 5 ("can't accept criticism" "I get in a rage")
      F. Etc, etc. = 9 (Two examples: "my past is my present" "I can't get close to anyone")

Comment: Although there is a wide range of responses to the above questions, some slight trends emerge. There is a recognition that to question 29 (What I don't understand about me) half of the group recognized lack of attaining their goal; others (8) indicated why they did what they did (My behavior). When the question becomes more focussed in question 49 (My problem is), there is a wider spread of replies. Perhaps surprising, some (6) pointed to their lacking trust. Others pointed to their sexual behavior; others to anger and rage. The remainder of the group were more general in their responses:

"myself" (5) and "my mind" (5).

In brief, this group of prisoners are, for the most part, recognizing their behavior and attempts are made to overcome their feelings.

A PRISONER'S RESPONSE TO QUESTION 49, "I MANIPULATE"

One prisoner's response to question 49 was "I manipulate." This he brought up in group therapy. Following two intense sessions, in which he became angry and filled with projections, we finally had him looking at himself. His entire PET is in Appendix I, Example 2. This is what he wrote after the above session:

> I want what I want when I want it. I didn't care how I got it, just so I got it. This has been my attitude all my life, whether I had to lie or manipulate. I didn't care who I hurt. I did this the last time I was out of prison.
>
> I knew that I was out of my comfort zone and for me to get back into that zone I would have to do something to come back to prison where it was more comfortable. In my mind I was blaming everyone but myself for why I came back to prison. If it wasn't for my victim's identifying me as the one who robbed them I would not be here today. When I was on the streets, I had the attitude that I was better than everyone else. When I was drinking, I felt powerful and in control like I had everyone on a string and they were at my beck and call and like I had control over everyone else and I would show them who was boss. I was on a self-destructive crash course and I wanted to take as many people as I could down with me. I just did not care. By me blaming everyone for my problems, it was a cop out and it helped me to get back into my comfort zone. I had graduated from two programs but only 'cause I had to and it gave me brownie points with my P.O. and I felt as though I had him wrapped around my little finger. The programs really didn't do me any good cause I still got angry and drank all because I did not want to face my problems and I was in my comfort zone. I was a very self-centered person.

To all appearances this appears to be a "breakthrough," an insight, and an acceptance. The proof, of course, will come when he leaves prison.

Chapter 5

FAIRY TALES: PRISONERS' REPLIES

I was first introduced to fairy tales early in life. My mother not only read to us children from the typical fairy tales, she was an excellent teller and creator of fairy tales of her own. I loved her fairy tales best. In the afternoon, Mom would "spin out" her enchanting fairy tale just before naptime. It made napping and dreaming so much more pleasant. Bettelheim (1976) noted that Goethe credited his mother's fairy tale telling and their own shared ideas as a provider for future self-confidence.

Much later, after I became a clinical psychologist, I began to utilize with selected alcoholic patients (Scott, 1970) a few lines from Williams's (1981) The Velveteen Rabbit. The lines used were those of the Skin Horse telling the Velveteen Rabbit how he became real: "The boy's uncle made me real" (p. 16). The Velveteen Rabbit, as so many patients, wanted to know if it hurt, and did it happen all at once. In my experience, the Skin Horse, as do successful patients, remarked that it was worth the "price."

Years later, as my experience and confidence grew with prisoners in group therapy, I began to reflect on the clinical wisdom of using fairy tales, myths, and fables with them. I was certain that these ideas needed to be gradually introduced into the ongoing group agenda. We did not dispense with reality–life in prison: how was the past week, did they receive lock-up time, good or bad news, etc. Once this was attended to, then the "luxury" of Greek myths and fairy tales would be utilized. Upon reflection, it was decided that selected Greek myths would potentially provide an introduction to fairy tales.

I felt that Oedipus would be an excellent introduction to Greek myths. I believe it can be accurately stated that this was Freud's favorite. I took liberty with Oedipus. Following Sophocles's (1971) *Oedipus Rex*, his next drama was *Oedipus at Clonus* (1971). In this drama, Oedipus struggled with guilt. Utilizing defenses to their fullest, he reasoned that the killing (of his father) was in self-defense. Secondly, this fate was decreed by the gods before his birth.

I took liberty with *Oedipus at Clonus*, and employing a modern punishment, had him placed in prison for killing his father and having intercourse with his mother. Moreover, this news was learned by the other prisoners. Their reactions can be found in Scott's (1994) "Oedipus Among Prisoners?" Among the responses were "I'd kill myself" and "He'd be beaten–Oedipus was beaten" (p. 278). A lively discussion preceded and followed in which very deep feeling responses emerged from the group members. Following this clinical success, other Greek myths were selected for discussion.

The utilization of Greek myths had been quite successful for prison group therapy as noted. Now it was judged the fairy tales could be introduced. There have been but few articles in the professional literature regarding crime and fairy tales. An exception is that of Meuller (1986). In his article "The Criminological Significance of Grimms' Fairy Tales," Meuller wrote, "Virtually every tale in the Grimm collection contains a message of law–not necessarily criminal law–of justice, punishment or pardon" (p. 217).

GERMAN WORD *MAEVE* MEANS MESSAGE

Meuller pointed out that the word tales is from *Murchen*, which in turn is derived from "the High German word *Maeve*, denoting messages that are important to be remembered" (p. 218). Hence, the term fairy tales might be more appropriately called *Volken* (folk) *Murchen* (messages). Although *Volken Murchen* is the more appropriate name, we will retain the more popular, though less correct, name of fairy tales. In fact, Bettelheim (1976) reflected, "It is unfortunate that both the English and French names for these stories emphasize the role of fairies in them–because in most no fairies appear" (p. 26).

Not all authors have agreed with Meuller's idea regarding the purpose of fairy tales. Heuscher (1963), in his book *A Psychiatric Study of Fairy Tales*, argued, "Many fairy tales and myths, as we have seen, deal with the evolution of the human child and humanity with particular stress upon the spiritual (as contrasted with the material) aspect of this evolution" (p. 194). The difference between Meuller and Heuscher can be observed in the emphasis in Cinderella. The former noted the severity of punishment, while the latter suggested the loss of eyes to the stepmother and stepsisters–pecked out by white birds "illustrates the progressive loss for the spiritual" (p. 194).

Before proceeding further, either definitions or descriptions of fairy tales are in order. Bettelheim (1976) has provided various notions regarding fairy tales. He wrote, "The fairy tale is therapeutic because the patient finds his own solutions" (p. 25). In my opinion, Bettelheim's ideas regarding evil and its attraction appear to be especially appropriate for prisoners. He stated, "In fairy tales evil is as omnipresent as virtue" and "evil is not without its attractions" (p. 9).

Heuscher (1963) has stressed that fairy tales become involved in what "transcends our everyday reality" (p. 4) for which scientific methods are inadequate.

Huck (1979), in her discussion of modern fairy tales, selected Hans Christian Andersen as "the first author of modern fairy tales" (p. 249). Her evaluation of Andersen's work was that "every Andersen story bears his unmistakable stamp of gentleness, melancholy, and faith in God" (p. 249).

Contrasting fables with fairy tales, Bettelheim (1976) wrote, "Fables demand and threaten–they are moralistic" (p. 27). Whereas, he stated, "Myths typically involve superego demands in conflict with id motivated action" (p. 37).

As previously mentioned, Meuller had indicated a relation between crime and fairy tales, but he had not directly worked with prisoners. Holton (1995) is convinced that fairy tales offer a clinical application. It is his contention that, "In our search to find the approach that best facilitates adjustment by offenders–that engenders internalization of mainstream societal values–we seem to have overlooked a medium that has proven itself over centuries of use: fairy tales" (p. 210). Specifically, Holton, in his work with offenders, wrote, "The simple, story-telling, literary approach which characterizes most tales is compatible with the cognitive levels of most offenders" (p. 218). However, Holton did not indicate direct clinical data.

PRISONER RESPONSES TO: "ARE YOU REAL OR MECHANICAL?"

In view of what I termed "clinical success" of employing with alcoholics (Scott, 1970) the exchange between the Skin Horse and the Velveteen Rabbit (as noted previously), I chose this as an introduction to fairy tales with my prison groups. For these groups I read from Williams' (1981) *Velveteen Rabbit* pages 14 and 16, slowly, twice. When I finished, they were asked, "Are you real or mechanical?"

I recorded during group their various responses:

Group 1

Dave: I'm not real. I'm mechanical and don't feel, most of my life. I'd rather be real–feel and care. I need a lot of treatment.

Steve: I was real. I've become mechanical like my dad. I had fleeting emotions from mom and a grade school teacher in third grade. Now, I think I need to be close to a woman.

Ben: Real, I well, I'm hard. When little, my grandparents made me real. Then I was sent back home and started to become hard and mechanical and cared for no one. Treatment has helped. I care about my victims. I have a heart.

Steve: How do you feel?

Ben: I'm not sure.

Joe: In prison to have a heart means to be brave.

Dave: Yeah, a stand up person!

Ben: In the bottom of my heart, I love my grandparents. I'd do anything for them.

Sam: I've been real only around a few people. I'm mostly mechanical.

Jack: I'm not real. I don't care if I hurt someone.

Dr. Scott: Can any of you make yourselves real? Do you need someone else, like the Velveteen Rabbit?

Dave: I need someone. Treatment can do it. Like you, Dr. Scott. You make me think and look at myself.

Steve: I'm trying to be as real as I can.

Ben: Not only you, Dr. Scott, but all the group members help to make me real.

Sam: My trouble is to let people close enough to help me become real.

The reader can observe a wide range of responses, qualifications, and what appears to be helpful for the group members. Some of the highlights are the following:

1. Steve needs a woman to make him real. How accurate is this for the typical male?
2. Ben states that he has a heart that, shall we say, is a necessary ingredient to be real, but not a sufficient one.
3. Joe provides a realistic variable, namely in prison having a heart means to be brave. Perhaps many of the readers will be reminded of either the Tin Woodsman or the Cowardly Lion in Baum's (1972) *Wizard of Oz.* According to the fairy tale (or fantasy) the former lacked a heart, whereas the latter had a heart but not courage. It seems that the Tin Woodsman is the prisoner who tries to be mechanical. Whereas, the majority of these prisoners had a heart but similar to the Cowardly Lion were fearful.
4. Ben, the practical prisoner, using Joe's idea, said that outside of prison he has a heart for his grandparents. This is, Ben states, "at the bottom of his heart."
5. Sam's judgement is uncertain; he's a mixture. Shall we say Sam is typical of the characters in the *Wizard of Oz* who had to undergo dangers (problems) in order to help themselves. This theme is most applicable to prisoners in and out of prison. Each situation has a specific demand. Counseling, therapeutic insight and psycho education fails to provide, in and of itself, growth.
6. Dave indicated that I (Dr. Scott) had been helpful.
7. Ben adds the idea of group therapy–all members are therapists for each other.

The following week, the group was asked: "If you wanted to change, would you need to change your mind or your heart?"

Steve: Change of heart is longer. That is, my emotions are more difficult, to feel better toward myself. I hope

	when out and I get thinking of burglary, I feel it's wrong–then! At *that* moment.
Ben:	My mind. I get down in the dumps.
Joe:	That's feelings or emotion?
Ben:	Yeah, but I think at times, everyone is after me.
Dr. Scott:	When raping, were you feeling or thinking?
Ben:	Thinking.
Group:	What! (Laughter)
Ben:	(Silent)
Dr. Scott:	We'll come back to you.
Herb:	Heart. I get in trouble with my feelings. And I have to avoid anger.
Todd:	It's my mind that needs to change. I have a good heart and a bad mind.
Steve:	How about your molesting?
Todd:	I felt sex was dirty with my wife–after my molesting.
Sam:	Heart. For a long time I thought it was my mind. But it was a feeling. I felt lonely, I felt powerless. Only lately has it occurred to me. I was after feelings.
Jack:	Feelings. My heart. I fed off the girl's fear. I have to care if I'm going to change.
Ben:	Yeah, it was feelings. The penis. What I have to change is the feelings.

The reader will note some changes following the original responses the previous week:

1. Steve questions his "brave heart," either in or out of prison. He did, however, show some courage (the Cowardly Lion?) by confronting Todd.
2. Todd makes a distinction of having a good heart but a bad mind. We must question this assumption about him or others.
3. Sam has now changed from half and half to all heart.
4. Ben comes clean–it's sexual feelings. It is most likely that this strong sex drive and his molesting and raping provides a backdrop for his paranoid orientation. In prison these two crimes are at the bottom of the prison pecking order. This is a real challenge for Ben. So far he's chosen only spurts of courage.

Group 2

Joe: I don't let people love me. An ex-girlfriend did me in. My heart, at the bottom of my heart I'm scared of life.

Jim: I'm mechanical. I've hurt too many people. And I get hurt too. I'm lonely. I'd like to be real. I went to AA and NA, but afterwards I drank or used. I'm, well, real in my cell.

Luke: I think I'm real. I'm loved by people and I hurt. Yet, I'm most real in this group therapy. I, uh, we deal with things we should.

Dr. Scott: What's at the bottom of your heart?

Luke: Anger, hate and fear. Uh, well, fear is the deepest. It's always there.

Joe: We all have fear.

Luke: Yeah, but mine is always there.

Fred: I'm mechanical, mostly. It's safe that way. I'm afraid to be real.

Joe: My mom treated me like hell. And so did my girl friends and my brother. Hell, the bikers treated me better than anyone. In church, I got kicked out. I told the minister that I heard voices.

Jim: I don't have an excuse. I just got sick of my parents. Emotionally I'm about 15 years old. I'm not mad at religion. I'm spiritual.

Luke: Fear can kill you. I can take only so much. I'd commit suicide instead of waiting and waiting for them or him to do it.

Jim: There's one of the Proverbs that says "Give a man strong drink."

Luke: Wouldn't help. I know Isaiah, I think, it's verse, well, no, it says, "Fear not."

Joe: My mom is now doing well. I hate it! Grandma has talked to me several times, although she's dead. That's what I told the minister.

Dr. Scott: Do it now. Let Grandma talk to you.

Joe: No. I don't want Grandma to know I'm in prison.

Luke: I thought you didn't care about anything.

Dr. Scott: Open your heart to Grandma.

Joe:	I won't.
Luke:	I have awful dreams every night, almost every night.
Dr. Scott:	Let's see if you can have good dreams. Try until next week's group.
Luke:	It won't work.

At this point Luke produced a complex and complicated drawing of his experienced condition. Time ran out and the group had to terminate. Luke's artwork suggested rather clearly that he is trapped in his own thinking and feeling processes. In short, Luke is a prisoner of his own heart.

Note that Joe indicated several personality characteristics: (1) fear; (2) a type of sponge personality which soaks up everything; and (3) refusal to use hypnosis which would potentially put him in contact with Grandma. Joe reminds one of a type the Velveteen Rabbit mentioned who questioned, "Does it hurt?"

Fred has given up being real. He chose to be mechanical. This he attempted to practice six months after the above statement.

Several significant clinical issues emerged, one being where is one real? Jim chose his cell, while Luke chose the group. Yet, Luke has such strong fears and is confused as clearly indicated by his drawing. Incidentally, he did report a good dream the following week.

The reader will observe the rather quick change in clinical practice, a sort of changing signals at the "line of scrimmage"–namely, hypnosis. The data that emerges is significant. Usually the clinical tactic is so sudden, the patient-prisoner doesn't have time to organize his defenses.

The following week, in an effort to further the previous week's reflections and to extend it, the group was asked: "If you wanted to change, would you need to change your mind or your heart?"

Luke:	For me, it's my heart. I can change my mind but not how I feel. I tried it by not letting it bother me, to have my mind blank it out, but it's still there.
Dr. Scott:	Why not change your heart?
Luke:	I can't. In my heart, buried deep in my heart, when I was a kid I was taught to love and trust. Then my dad leaves. I was young.
Joe:	I'd have to change my heart. It goes beyond my mind, then spills out in my head.

Dr. Scott:	How rid yourself of this problem?
Joe:	No idea.
Fred:	For me, it's my mind. I let things take root. It's like an addiction. It is an addiction.
Luke:	It was a feeling. Wasn't it–of killing?
Fred:	No! Thinking!
Joe:	Well, at least it was a desire that was driving you, Fred.
Fred:	I didn't feel while I was killing. Afterwards I felt fear.
Dr. Scott:	Did you know you were killing?
Fred:	No.
Joe:	Did you care?
Fred:	No.
Luke:	I had, I felt hurt. I get hurt easily. I didn't know what I was doing in my killing.
Dr. Scott:	Why not witness it?
Luke:	I couldn't.
Joe:	Last week I said I hated my Mom. But this past week I've thought of her. I could love her.
Fred:	If I hadn't been caught, I'd have gone on, more killings. I didn't know how to stop.
Luke:	I want my victim to forgive me. At times in my cell I feel my dead victim's presence. Maybe my victim has come to haunt me.
Fred:	I'd like to connect with my victim's spirit. I might understand what my victim went through.

At this point group hypnosis was done. The reader will recall that when a procedure "gives way" to a more appropriate one, that procedure is employed. Luke did not participate. He stated that it was because of fear. Surprisingly, Fred did participate and reported, "I felt someone was near me." He was uncertain whether it was his victim. Fred, in his usual style, makes "infallible" statements (in this instance being mechanical) and compares this to an addiction which, in turn, gives way to the hypnotic technique. He reported that he felt "someone near."

What seems significant are the major differences between Fred and Luke (both murderers) regarding their basic orientations–mental or feeling–while performing their homicidal act.

Group 3

Gifford: Yep. I'm real. My son did it. I had to think of him and not just myself. (Unreal before?) Yeah. I was beaten by Dad. I hated him. Now I'm getting over it.

Dr. Scott: The story *The Velveteen Rabbit* spoke of once real, you can't become unreal. Can this be applied to being un-criminal? That is, if you become non-criminal, would it last for always?

Gifford: It could. I'm not thinking criminal.

Dr. Scott: What about your heart? Could it be criminal and your head non-criminal?

Gifford: My head controls my heart. A real criminal's heart is cold–don't give a shit.

Dr. Scott: What's a real criminal?

Gifford: I was.

Stephen: That's a tough question. I'm trying to be a real person, not a real criminal. Trying, that is, to get a hold of my emotions and thoughts.

Dr. Scott: Which is more important to get a hold of?

Stephen: Emotions.

Larry: I'm working on being real. I was mechanical–drugs and alcohol. I cared for nothing.

Bob: I see good in things, so I'm not mechanical.

Gifford: You gave up your kids. Is that caring? (That was a sharp remark, and I believe necessary to be made.)

Fritz: I'm often mechanical, when it serves my purpose. I was addicted to the big drugs for 20 years.

Dr. Scott: Ever un-addicted?

Fritz: All I've known is addiction. Hatred, anger, and violence in my heart. If anyone tried to manipulate me, it all boiled over.

Stephen: Fritz, you're from California–prisons are tough there. I was in prison in California.

Fritz: Prisons helped to make me mechanical.

Larry: I've been in the joint 21 years. My wall is finally crumbling.

Gifford: I've been in 16 years–my walls are crumbling. I used to see it as a sign of weakness.

Fairy Tales: Prisoners' Replies 55

Fritz: I'm getting tired of prison, though I'm caught between good and bad—and I waver.

From Larry and Fritz we learn two methods of their, and likely others', becoming mechanical. For Larry it was drugs and alcohol. For Fritz, it was prison life, but his son, according to him, is "making me real." Why not? If the boy's uncle made the Skin Horse real, why can't his son, appearing at the right time (like in a sunrise), help his father to be real?

Gifford provides what we hope is not true. Yet some evidence suggests that for the real criminal, the heart is cold. Do we have the tools to make this type of diagnosis? Gifford himself is not ready for release. He has made good statements ("My son made me real") and he doesn't think criminal anymore. But, Reader, wait until next week's group session.

What must alert us is Fritz's statement, "I'm often mechanical—when it serves my purpose." This strikes me as significant and true. I'm concerned that this statement accurately describes many other offenders.

How does Fritz, or any other prisoner (similar to Fritz with the same diagnosis) know when he will employ his "mechanical self?" What "turns on" the mechanical self?

The following week the group was asked, "If you decided to change, would the change need to be in your mind or heart?"

Bob: My mind tells me how to think, like not to be so paranoid, and feeling I'm picked on. If I had a normal mind, I'd see things correctly.

Larry: Feelings. I have to control my feelings, my emotions. My emotions take me over. Uh, since the fifth grade, all my anger, and since, uh...

Fritz: My mind. My perception. How I see things.

Gifford: I don't want to change.

Dr. Scott: Are you an offender saint?

Gifford: Yeah. No. When I did my killing, I got excited. I didn't care.

Dave (new member): It's my mind. That's my problem.

Stephen: My mind. The way I think. Doing my killing, I felt numb. But, there was some anger in there, somewhere. Yeah! Anger.

This group was composed of "heavy" prisoners, yet there were flashes of honesty–"I'm paranoid;" or "It's my mind," and "I'm mechanical," etc. Yet, Gifford, who the week before had made very positive feelings, now contradicts himself. Gifford had been in group two and a half years. He would alternate his emotions and his mind. Also, he would "play to the audience" and take an unpopular or a contrary stance. A variable, his consistent dream, made him a willing member of group. He disliked me for my insistence regarding the dream, yet "got hooked." His dream consisted of not being able to find his way out of a building following someone's death.

THE FISHERMAN AND THE GENIE: PROLONGED IMPRISONMENT INCREASES HATRED?

Following the clinical success of the prisoners in group therapy to *The Velveteen Rabbit*, it was decided to choose another fairy tale for presentation and discussion. The choice was *The Fisherman and the Genie*. Bettelheim (1976) had written, "According to adult morality, the longer an imprisonment lasts, the more grateful the prisoner should be to the one who liberates him" (p. 29). This would make, a priori, a most appropriate fairy tale for prisoners. The essential aspect of this fairy tale was read. In essence, the genie in the bottle would be most gracious to the person who freed it soonest. With longer imprisonment, the more and more angry the genie would become, saying to himself that whoever let him free, "him will I slay." The essential portion was read during group therapy, slowly, twice. The following are verbatim responses from two group therapies.

PRISONER RESPONSES

Group 1

Larry: I don't see myself as a victim. Well, some ways in prison. Uncomfortable. Not much tolerance. I don't speak, that's why I keep to myself, the crap, the trash talk. Sometimes I feel like a ghost. It's weird. I'd

	hate to die and be a real ghost and haunt people.
Bill:	A genie in the next life?
Larry:	I hope not, even a sex offender has some values.
Dennie:	I can't blame anyone but myself. I knew what I did was wrong, I didn't give a damn. I'm starting to see things. When I came to prison at first I was bitter.
Bill:	My crime–murder. I've indulged in self-punishment. I'm paranoid about death, I have to push it away. Another problem is hope. I've had it crushed so often. All these years in prison. It's all gone.
Red:	I've mellowed out. Age does it. When I was younger I was a bitter man. I couldn't take "no" from anyone. I was lucky I didn't kill someone.
Ray:	I'm more bitter now. Ten years, I hate all of prison. But, on outside I was tough. My crime, my murder has stuck in my mind–it's like a broken camera that keeps flashing the same picture over and over. I'm tough in prison.
Red:	It's a front, a cover to keep people at a distance. Ray, you're a cream puff. (Ray is silent.)
Red:	Are you?
Ray:	Yes.

In general this group did not agree with the lesson or moral of *The Fisherman and the Genie*. Two members claim not to be able to blame anyone but themselves. In a way, these two prisoners did not enter into the fairy tales, saying they put themselves in the bottle (prison).

One member (Bill) reflected on the factor that length of stay in prison (the bottle) crushed hope. In this sense, Bill has crossed over from a fairy tale to a Greek myth. Pandora was Epimetheus's wife. Epimetheus was the not so smart brother of Prometheus. Prometheus is well known for his bravery and kindness by stealing fire from the Olympian gods. Zeus, the chief god, was in a rage. Zeus gave Pandora a gift, a jar, which she was not to open. She did and out came all the evils and problems of the world. The one good gift was hope. We learn that years in prison had crushed even Pandora's one and only gift–hope. My impression of Bill (he had been in my group treatment for two years) was that he had lost his original anger. He did not forego all hope, but resorted to a special type of a hallucinatory life. We will read his own fairy tale in the next chapter.

In sharp contrast are Red and Ray. Red is older and mellowed. Ray is young (in late twenties) and stated that he is more bitter presently. It's my opinion that his misplaced target since his crime (murder) is likened to a broken camera lens. He relives his crime over and over. This, therefore, provides a factor not calculated in *The Fisherman and the Genie*. The Genie had done no crime, specifically not murder. Red seems to sense this and calls Ray a "cream puff." Ray has to admit this in front of the group–no easy task.

What complicates this fairy tale has to do with which version is used. The one read to them was that of a genie locked in a bottle by an evil giant. As Bettelheim (1976) noted, an older version from "Judean-Persian legends according to which King Solomon often imprisoned disobedient or heretic spirits in iron casts" (p. 312). The version read simply addressed itself to the effects of short-time versus long-term imprisonment.

Group 2

Tim: At first I hated everyone. I wanted to kill my family. They turned me in. But not now.

Albert: I was mad, but at myself. I'm not angry anymore. I was arrested, but as the saying goes, "I was arrested but rescued." Even my family thinks I'm improving. I'll never murder again. If I do it will be suicide. I'll kill myself.

Paul: Yeah. I was angry at first. In prison I got in with the wrong group. For a time lately I've been mad at the parole board. They gave me some hope, lately.

Terry: A short time ago, I told someone in this joint that I'd kill the judge and others. I was mad, mad, mad. Finally, I'm coming to the place that it's my fault.

Mike: I went through phases where I was pissed off at every one–lawyers, PO's, and the staff in prison. I wanted out.

Ted: At first I was angry and resentful at others.

Ron: I've been resentful all my life. It's the third time I've been locked up, and I'm only in my thirties. I've done a lot of crime. I'm damn mad at the woman who put me here.

The comments produced a wide range of responses. Ron appears most like the Genie. Instead of being angry at the giant who put him in prison, he places his finger "on the woman who put me here." Ron was a new member to the group. Hopefully he will "mature out" as did Terry. This dynamic, the dynamic of hate, must go. If it doesn't, this type of prisoner is a threat upon release.

In summary, the dominant opinion seems to be anger at first, followed by a "maturing out," or "growing up." This in turn allows, maybe for the first time, the prisoner to question why he really is in prison.

BETTELHEIM'S THESIS: PARTLY FAILED

In our opinion, Bettelheim's (1976) thesis failed. Part of the problem was that after his opening statement of "adult morality," he applied the fairy tale to that of a child and his (big) father. Another reason is, it seems to me, Bettelheim had not worked directly with prisoners. Bettelheim's psychoanalytic approach, too generously (or overgenerously) applied, fails regarding this particular population.

REFLECTIONS

As the title of this book suggests, for some prisoners it is a struggle of the heart (emotions), while for other prisoners, it is a battle with their minds (thinking). Still, for most prisoners, it is a turmoil for both their emotions (heart) and thinking (mind). The presented clinical exercise has provided some very fruitful material, not only for discussion but much more significantly, it touched (really touched) the heart and mind of most of the prisoners. Some rather rare insights, troubling emotions, and reflections emerged.

Chapter 6

FAIRY TALES BY PRISONERS

These groups had been prepared by Greek myths and responses to fairy tales. It was now their turn to become creative and write a fairy tale of their own. Years earlier, without preparation, the groups were introduced to Boethius's (1986) *Consolation of Philosophy*. A brief history of Boethius was given: A man who lived A.D. 480-524 became a Roman prisoner and was beheaded. He found relief in prison when he wrote and reflected on philosophy. The groups produced no stories. Perhaps it was too realistic and therefore too challenging. Fairy tales were, it seemed, an avenue for creativity. The response was exceptional. Six fairy tales have been chosen for this book. The prisoners were given two weeks to write a fairy tale. All but one prisoner wrote a fairy tale. He could not write but was an active verbal member of the group.

FAIRY TALE 1: THE TALE OF ANAK THE GIANT AND THE SYLPH

by Bill

The bearing of Anak by the Great Mother was a painful ordeal because Anak had a great fall to Aretz, the name of our planet that we care for now. Anak wandered our lands for 200 years and sometimes would sit on a large rock and weep, for he was very lonely. He could find no mate or people who would accept him, for they didn't want to feed or clothe him because of their great need to feed and clothe themselves. Anak finally gave up the fight for survival; he decided to starve himself to death so he would never again feel that awful rejection of people around him. He was finding it hard to find a place befitting for a giant to die, so he asked an old man he saw on the edge of the path where such a place may be. The old man replied, "You will come to a river in the south, if you continue on this path. Follow it until you come to a dark wood. You must walk to the center of the wood where there is a spring coming from the ground. There you may rest a while or forever if you wish it so." Then Anak the Giant nearly ran down the path and found the river and followed it until he came to the dark wood. It looked like a terrible, scary place to die, yet as he entered it, he had the feeling of peace and tranquility, almost like love was exuding from it. He walked a path that took him deeper into the dark wood and he came to a grove, and in the center of it was a large spring bubbling from it. There appeared a beautiful sylph with transparent butterfly wings. She looked at Anak and said, "Why have you come to my grove, Great Giant?" Anak replied, "I have come to die; I have walked 200 years and found no one to love. Will you stay with me?" The sylph said, "Yes, and you may call me Dee-Dee, and I'm sure you know the law of the Great Mother, that you can't murder yourself by your own hand, that you must live on until you die naturally. Drink of my spring and rest and I shall give you a present while you sleep."

So Anak lay down, and after pondering the law of the Great Mother and wondering if Dee-Dee would be around when he woke up, he went to sleep. In the dream of Anak, there came a very beautiful young woman with blond locks and a very short nightgown, just covering her blouse. She was embarrassed because Anak was looking at her with very approving eyes. When Anak awoke and looked around the grove, he could not find Dee-Dee, and he sat down and started to weep again. Suddenly there was a whisper inside of him, from his left side, and the whisper said, "I love you, it's alright, I am Dee-Dee and I am your mate. We are husband and wife and I am weeping with you because I am so happy. Will you be happy too?" Anak said yes he would be very happy with Dee-Dee, and that he had abandoned the idea of committing suicide because of the law that Dee-Dee had relayed to him. His newfound Goddess would go with him on his travels and would never have to return to the grove.

Dee-Dee showed Anak a hidden wooden flute in the grove and how to blow a certain tune on it to make food appear on the ground before him so he wouldn't have to dig for yams and potatoes to survive any longer. Even though he broke the law by starving himself almost to death, he was saved by the goddess and was given two wonderful gifts: marriage and a magical flute. So, when he told others of the Valley of the Shadow of Death, he always added the love and gentleness that he had found there and that he was doing a life-long penance for almost killing himself and that he would work with any person for free for serving his term in life. He would always whisper a song for the goddess before he went to sleep and she would always create a dream for Anak with her in it so he would never forget what she looked like or how much they loved each other. "The goddess is the Mother of our soul and She would never let us harm it or its body with our own hand." Ask Her to be sure!

REFLECTION

Bill's fairy tale, "The Tale of Anak the Giant and Dee-Dee the Sylph," is rather well done. We could term it a romantic fairy tale. Lacking love, Anak was ready to starve himself to death. By good fortune he met Dee-Dee, "a beautiful sylph," whose love saved him. He was willing to pay the price by his tears. The method of dreaming was a device to short-cut considerable adult thinking.

An added fairy tale trick was the "hidden wooden flute" that provided food for Anak. One is reminded of the Chinese fairy tale, *The Magic Flute*. In turn, Mozart's last opera, *The Magic Flute*, was, as explained by Solomon (1995), in the end more powerful than anger and bloodshed.

Anak is saved from a hopeless situation by Dee-Dee's love. We recall that from Pandora's box out came all the evils of the world, but hope remained. If one wanted to employ "unrealistic fantasy," one could say that Dee-Dee was Pandora. In reality, Bill was the prisoner who was able to "recapture" hope after it slid out of his mind. In summary, hope is hydra-headed, for good.

During group sessions Bill had related his friendship with Dee-Dee. In his words, "She's the only thing I have to hold on to." After some exchange among other members of the group, Bill related, "I'm sick and tired of reaching out to convicts. All they want to do is sneak around. I get lonely and cry." Bill was asked why he didn't reach out to the staff. His response was, "No. It's a power game. All they want is information."

Bill might not be exactly accurate about this last statement. He does indicate an effort not to identify with "the convicts," whose goal is to sneak around. This demands a price. In Bill's words, "No one hardly knows me anymore. I've let go of so many people in prison. They weren't good for me." Four members of the group agreed with Bill on this last point. One member indicated, "Having no one is terrible."

At this juncture I've an hypothesis: Bill's female friend (Dee-Dee) suggests that their phenomenon is not so much a psychotic phenomenon as it is an imaginary playmate. Not only child psychologists and psychiatrists are familiar with the occurrence. Many parents have learned from their children that they have an imaginary playmate. Bill's "friend" seems to function at this level. Prison life presents the typical TO, which is Winnicott's (1953) transitional object. The imaginary "playmate" is a substitute. During several sessions we have asked, "When are you real?" The two most usual places are "In my cell" or "In group."

Finally, Bill added, "The meds didn't remove her out of my mind." Bill did require meds, but according to him, psychotropic medication did not eliminate "my friend."

FAIRY TALE 2: THE LITTLE PONY

by Ted

There was once a little boy who dreamed of owning a little pony, a pony to call his own to befriend and ride whenever he chose, to be free to escape into a world beyond fantasy. The little pony would fulfill all the mystical fantasies of play that a little boy cherishes in his heart. The dream was always a source of joy and excitement, the happiness an overwhelming emotion filled with fun, fantasy, play, and laughter. The summer was always like that, thought the boy.

The winter seemed endless as the boy stared out the window into a cold white blanket of snow covering the landscape of a shallow creek in the meadows with an unblemished background of snow-covered hills.

It was during the fall season the boy drummed up the courage to ask his father for the little pony. "Maybe," answered his father with a smile. Yes, a maybe is better than a no and the undisguised smile was the clincher, thought the boy rationally. Perhaps now the dream of owning the little pony would come true.

Shortly before summer, however, the boy's father had grown seriously ill with a disease and passed away. Cancer of some sort, they called it, but the whispers echoed in the hallway. The loss of his father was a tremendous blow in his life leaving the boy sad, lonely, afraid and withdrawn, and the dream of the little pony was a fading childhood memory.

As the little boy grew into a young man, life as he knew it would change dramatically. One day as the young man was playing in the meadows he came to stand before a beautiful four-legged, solid-hoofed animal with flowing mane and tail, its great strength, its snorting with its large nostrils, its pawing the ground in impatience, its excitement at the prospect of battle, and its not being terrified by the clashing of weapons. A white horse, a stallion of characteristic strength, pure, clean, righteous, and prepared for warfare patiently waiting to be mounted. And yet the fiery eyes of the white horse depicted a different warfare unseen by the young man. Intrigued by the awesome beauty of the animal he immediately equipped it with a bridle, reins, saddlecloth and saddle, and with an air of dignity of a horseback rider he swiftly mounted the horse using the bridle and whip to control it.

The dream of the little pony had come true after all. The doors to a world of fantasy were opened. A wonderful opportunity to fulfill the lost dreams of a little boy. A noble gallant fighting for the honor of a maiden, a cowboy, sheriff or Billy the Kid. What a daring thought, an Indian war chief, perhaps, maybe a civil war hero, or a medieval warrior slaying three-headed dragons or a mythical god on a flying horse. Yes, laughed the young man joyfully. The fantasies were endless.

The young man led the animal into the meadows with a steady galloping pace. The rider experienced a sense of power, control and confidence, coupled with a feeling of euphoria unbeknown to man. The rider now confident quickened the pace of the stride and rode the white horse hard with an intensity so powerful that the exhilarating speed of the animal consumed the passion of his heart. The young man had fallen in love. Each ride was a new experience, a new fantasy to conquer but with each ride an evil purpose began to surface.

Aware of the evil presence the young man threw fear into the wind and cautiously approached the white horse but did not mount. Today he will not ride. The desire to ride, however, burned silently in his soul. The animal waited patiently knowing the rider would soon ride again.

Awakened from a deep sleep drenched in sweat the young man awoke terrified and shaken trying desperately to make sense of the dream. They came at night like they always do between the hours of two (2) and four (4) A.M. No two dreams were ever alike except at the end of each dream are two (2) lights of scarlet color glowing in the distance. The dream tonight was horrible. A beast, faceless, ugly and grotesque was seen rising from a pit of hell, the body, thin-fleshed and wretched in pain, an evil mind fueling the fury of hate into a cold, unfeeling heart. Evil and menacing were the eyes of the beast, calculating dark, cold and empty. But it was beyond the horrifying stare of the beast that beheld a disturbing shadow flickering in the darkness.

Another night another dream. The vision beheld a devastating tornado in turmoil violently whirling throughout the land destroying everything in its path, children, women, and man. And out of the dust emerged a lethal power of destruction, a second beast, a predator of mankind. But it was the eyes, always the eyes. In the eyes of the beast lay the shadow unnerving and haunting.

Exhausted and losing the battle to fend off sleep, the young man drifted frightened and nervous in and out of sleep until finally a deep sleep overcame him. His mind and body tossed and turned in fearful anticipation. Silently in the night it came. The dream.

In the midst of clouds I saw a human head with a flame burning in its body suspended in time and space. The head oscillating to and fro as though it were saying "No." The facial features undefined for the head was faceless. The eyes unexpressionable yet crying. Something in the mouth, what is it? Strange the mouth held a bit attached to a bridge. What does it mean, what does the dream mean?

And there it was, movement, the shadow was stirring in the eyes of the head. The shadow now beckoned the young man. As he stared deeply into the darkness of the eyes he trembled with fear at the horror before him and the realization struck him all at once, "My God, Noooo . . ." The scream pierced the night.

From out of the darkness stepped forward a beast, faceless, ugly and grotesque, shackled in chains with a bit and bridge in its mouth, the eyes no longer calculating, dark, cold or empty, but rather resigned, tormented, and pleading. A flame endlessly burning in its soul consuming its heart with an obsession of selfish desire. A beast of burden. And in the distance of the dream the fiery eyes of scarlet color taunted and laughed at the pitiful creation of its control. The white horse knowing the young man would ride again. The beast of burden now has a face. The old man wept. The nightmare was over. Deeply imbedded in the memory of a little boy lies a forgotten dream of the little pony.

REFLECTION

Ted's fairy tale, "The Little Pony," begins with a dream; perhaps he means a daydream or a wish. The little pony had to be magical, not an ordinary horse since he would ride it "into a world beyond fantasy." That's a big order. Is it impossible? The little boy used this dream as a source of all his enjoyment.

Then reality sets in. He asks his father who smiled in favor. This dream was crushed when his father died. Yet, as a young man, magic did produce a horse, but a different and a most challenging horse with "fiery eyes." This horse was the center of his pleasure. Some investigators believe there is no location for true love and pleasure. Folklore does suggest a center or source of pleasure in the brain. Yet pleasure–really it was evil–got out of hand. A "deep sleep," although painful, did produce, eventually, insight followed by realistic action. Ted closed his fairy tale with this thought, "Deeply imbedded in the memory of a little boy lies a forgotten dream of the little pony."

This fairy tale Ted related concerns itself with his years of drug abuse and dependence. It is beautifully written with analogy. We might remark, this dream's thesis is a most modern one, that of drug dependence. It would be, we believe, most useful to reread Ted's fairy tale knowing that its theme is that of drug dependence.

It is noteworthy that both Bill and Ted utilize dreams as an important variable in their fairy tales. Bettelheim (1976) has written, "Many fairy tale heroes, at a crucial point in their development, fall into deep sleep . . ." (p. 214). Following the dream "a higher stage of maturity or understanding" (p. 214) occurs.

FAIRY TALE 3: THE TIME MACHINE

by Bob

Once upon a time in a far away land called Dematra sat a little boy. He seemed to be a sad little boy so I went over there to find out what was wrong and he told me his family deserted him and kicked him out on the streets. We got to talking and I told him a little about how as a kid I would be rejected and picked on and my family didn't want to have anything to do with me. He then began to ask me how I dealt with it and I told him I just ran away from home and got caught up in a tornado and it landed me here in the Land of Dematra and he was so amazed his eyes were like quarters. I asked what his name was and he said Stimpy and I told him my name was Bob and we became friends from then on. I told him that it sure would be nice to be a little boy again and Stimpy told me he can make that happen and he said "follow me" so I did and he told me to get inside this giant time machine and I did and within about three minutes I came out as a seven year old boy and it was so cool cuz I could relive my childhood over but with lots of happiness. Then Stimpy began to show me around the Land of Dematra. All I seen were little kids having a good time and he told me they were all full grown people at one time but they took a ride in the time machine and it brought them back twenty plus years in their life cause these had all been abused kids at one time and they decided that they wanted to relive their childhood over and I thought that this was pretty cool cause I had an abusive childhood as well and I could relate. So I just blended in with the crowd and felt at ease. This land of Dematra was cool cause there was no violence nor any drunk dads to beat on their kids or wives. There was beautiful positive music all around. The birds were chirping. The food was excellent. Homemade lasagna.

REFLECTION

Bob did not give his fairy tale a name; the one above has been suggested.

This fairy tale is, we believe, unique. It is a deeply wished desire to have another chance at childhood. Although the term "Time Machine" is new, Bob employed an old avenue to arrive in Dematra: a tornado.

There are some points in the fairy tale that are unclear or inconsistent. Stimpy, the little boy in Dematra, was "a sad little boy." If he were sad, why hadn't he used the "Time Machine?" Or, had he used it and the effects wore off? In all probability, this was simply a slip (error) in Bob's fairy tale.

I know Bob rather well. He is a childish young adult male who has refused to grow up, both in life and in fantasy.

FAIRY TALE 4: A MODERN DON QUIXOTE

by Don

I know where there's a secret place not too far from here. It's deep in the woods and a mystery to all except those who play. It's enchanted in a childish sort of way, for the special people who come here to play and come in all sorts of shape and sizes: canabals, animals and even a bigfoot or two. They come from all around, far and near for this is a special sort of playground for a certain time of year. It has a mountain for the king and caves and tunnels for people who are into that sort of thing. Roads and trails and a small little town. But beware of the clown for his idea of a joke may leave you on the ground. The town itself is a nice sorta place where everyone busily hurries around preparing for the night's party to take place. The Bards are tuning their harps and reciting the night's tales to be told in the Great Hall. The jugglers and jests are bouncing around barely able to hold their glee for the night to be. The sargent at arms and his men of might parade around for all who come to see, be it man, creature, or beast who comes to play. You must behave or be made to pay. The sun is setting and people, things, and animals are showing by the score in crowds, gangs and crews for the night ahead in this small little town. Some see friends, lovers, and faces they've never seen before. It's all fine and good. This party is sure to be better than the one before, and as the sun has fallen away it's time for this town's favorite part of the day and as the Great Hall doors swing away. The crowds go in their way walkin, crawlin, flyin. Upon going in, the sight they behold is of the stories to be told grandchildren when the nights grow long and cold. The tables are long and piled high with food from every walk of life, bowls, platters and baskets filled with delights and a fireplace glowing with warmth and light. From the rafters swing banners, flags and string left over from the little sparrows just this last spring. Paintings on the walls of old and new, people, creatures, places and in racks below sits cages of brandies, wines, beers that bring smiles and cheers from the crowds within. The host who never seems to grow old raises his stein letting everyone know the party's begun and a party it is. With dancing and tumblers and jugglers, always the fool, the Jest running, jumping. The Bards with songs of Joy. The wine flows free, guests enjoy the wine. With ease food consumed with steins of beer. Little brown colles seem to make people happier. As the party swings into full gear so do the party clowns who've had too much brandy and beer. Snow White's dancing on a table to a crowd's cheers and leers. When there was a cry of fright for "ol" Frankenstein and Big Foot have got in a drunken fight. Flyin went the tables and chairs. The next thing you know the whole place is in a drunken brawling fight with rebel yells and rows of might. Big Foot crossed out "ol" Frankenstein with left hook followed with an overhand right. The lights went out for Frankenstein that night and Big Foot headed for the doors grabbin a hold of Snow White in his rush. He knew any minute there was gonna be a very big bust. He made the street, feet hittin the dust, skidding to a halt beside his custom made Hog, settin White on the pad and with a prayer and then kickover his Hog, hopin the damn thing wouldn't bogg and with a thunder customary of a Hog his bike came to life and "ol" Big Foot rode off into the night.

REFLECTION

The author did not give his fairy tale a name. The one above is suggested.

This fairy tale begins as a joyful occasion for all types of people. There is a sergeant at arms. Is this a reminder of the guards at prison, regardless of the occasion, or does it suggest, regardless of where one is, a time for fun can get out of hand? A time for fun loosens self-control, and control from the outside is required.

There is an initial delight, "all is fine and good," reflecting a child's delight. Don, however, adds an adult's ingredient: alcohol. Don was an alcoholic and drugger. He, seemingly, can't willingly divorce himself from these stimulants that produce an ASC (altered state of consciousness). The fun begins in earnest; even Snow White is there. At the height of the good time comes the dramatic moment for conflict, a fight, a drunken brawl begins between "ol Frankenstein and Big Foot." A real western cowboy brawl. Eventually Big Foot wins. Now enters the modern Don Quixote. On the way out (after his victory), Big Foot grabs Snow White (unbelievable for the real Don Quixote). Instead of riding off on Rocinante, Big Foot jumps on his "Hog" (bike) and "rides off in the night" (with Snow White), although Don Quixote, as written by Cervantes (1958), would never have allowed Don Quixote to grab (kidnap?) Dulcinea and ride off with her.

This Don, in his fairy tale, allows himself this modern permission. Another modern aspect is that "our Don" has no help, as did Don Quixote with Sancho Panza. So goes "up-to-date" life—both real and in fairy tales!

The author of this fairy tale is an aggressive, fun-loving male. Our Don would have been wiser to take Dulcinea in the real Don Quixote story. Unaware of Dulcinea he chooses Snow White.

FAIRY TALE 5: ALL MUSIC: A REPLACEMENT FOR THE MAGIC FLUTE?

by Mike

There was once a young boy who always liked music, and one day thought he would be real famous. Each year he would play a different instrument. He played well. He loved all kinds of music. He would listen to it for hours. He played in school bands. By the fifth grade he was known as the only fifth grader to play the most instruments. People used to love to hear him play. Both of his parents were well known in the music business. The worked with him daily. He never got tired of practicing. Over the next few years, he had won awards for his playing. The piano, the violin, the saxophone. Other instruments of his choice. By the time he was in his high school years, he was into writing his own style of music. After he was out of high school, he decided to go to college to further his studies in music. While there, he wrote many musical pieces. By the age of 20 he was conducting his own band. His name got out and he was asked to play at several classical concerts. He became famous and rich.

One day the bad news came. Both of his parents were in a plane crash and were not seen since. Depression set in; and with that came a change in his music. Sales went down. He turned to drinking. Dealing with the loss of his parents was more than he could bare. He tried hard, but his music wasn't quite the same. He was sure he would never be the same again. He was at his all time low. Five years went by and nothing. One hot day of summer, in July, he was sitting in the hot sun, trying to piece his world back together when the ringing of the phone disrupted his thoughts. Upon answering the phone he found it to be a long distance call. It was the American Embassy from another country. His parents' plane went down in a densely populated part of the country. They have been unable to be moved due to the nature of their injuries. They were to be making it into the country within a few days. He was never so happy. He had a lot to do to prepare for their return. In the back of his mind, he knew that one day he would hear something about the disappearance of his folks. Now his parents are back. He is back to writing music and now he teaches music in the local high school. He still gets the chance to conduct with the high school band and with the college band. He's now married and has a few kids of his own. On those cool nights, when all is quiet, you can still hear the faint sound of music. He looks at his wife and knows that his children are going to be just like him.

The End . . .

REFLECTION

Music is Mike's love and his life, but so (more so) are his parents. Mike is a young man and most successful in his musical abilities. Then with the news of the loss of his parents in a plane wreck, he quickly goes into a deep depression and stops playing music. He begins to abuse alcohol. The depression had a lasting effect for five years.

Upon hearing that his parents were not dead but had been lost in the jungle, he quickly recovers. He begins to play music again, marries, and has children "that are going to be just like him." Does this last statement imply a neurotic dependency—as he has? It also suggests a nongenetic basis for alcohol, at least for the neurotic dependent personality.

Solomon (1995) has given the opinion in his book, *Mozart*, that, "In the end, music remained Mozart's primary talisman against corruption, fear, and death" (p. 517). Yet, Mozart had a struggle of independence against his dominating father. Did music help?

FAIRY TALE 6: LITTLE RED RIDING HOOD: THE TRUE STORY AS TOLD BY THE WOLF

by Tony

I would like to set the story stray [straight] as to what happen with little red riding hood and I. I an [am] the wolf. And this is what happened on that day.

Little Red Riding Hood was not going to grandma's house, and she did not have a basket of goodies. She was writing in the dirt. She was not waring [wearing] a red cape and hood. She was wearing shorts and tee shirt.

It was a sunny day in September. I was helping the landlord put screens on his windows. It gets cold at nights but it is still very hot in the daytime. We had just got done and I was going back to my trailer. When I saw this little girl (Little Red Riding Hood) setting writing in the dirt. So as I walked by her I lood [looked] down at what she was writing. She was writing something about loving some boy. It meant nothing to me, so I step around her and headed for my den. Hoping she would follow me.

She said, "Where are you going?" as she is getting up to walk with me.

"To my place," I say.

She said, "I am going to ride my bike," as she got on the bike and starts to ride along beside me. I am thinking that if she comes into my den I am going to take her.

We did not talk until we got to my place. As I walk across the yard she said, "I will ride around and park my bike." I went into my den and left the door open hoping that she would come in on her own. She did. I close the door. And the way the door closed it was hard to open, so I know she would not be able to open it without help.

"I have a friend who has a set of those," she says as she is pointing at my chess set. The chess peaces [pieces] are old whiskey bottles that look like chess peaces [pieces].

I say, "I wish I had them all. Has your friend got all of them?"

"Yes, he does," she says as she is looking around at the inside of my den.

"Would you like a look around or have you been in here before?" I ask, hoping to get her back into the bedroom.

"Yes, I have been in here before, but you can show me around if you want to," she says as she starts to walk through my trailer. My trailer is not all that big so the living room and the kitchen she could tell what they are. The next room was my junk room then the bathroom and then the bedroom. As Red is standing by the dresser and I am sitting on the couch, she says, "You have small eyes."

"All the better to see you with in the dark," I say.

"O' what a long tongue you have," she says.

"All the better to eat you with," I says.

"How are you going to eat me with your tongue," she asks, "and not your teeth?"

So I stand up and put a hand over her mouth. "Do not scream," I tell her as I am laying her down on my bed. Then I take her shorts and under paints [pants] off of her and spread her legs.

"This is how," I say as I show her. When I am done doing that I stand up and take my paints [pants] and shorts off.

"O' what is that big thing for?" she asks.

"I am going to show you," I say as I am getting down on her. When I am done and let her get up she puts her under paints [pants] and shorts back on. We go back out into the living room. I stop her at the door. "You are not going to tell anyone are you?" I ask.

She says, "No, I won't tell anyone," and she leaves.

After she is gone I lay down and go to sleep. I wake up to someone at the door. It is the cop. Thay [they] come in and cut my tool [penis] off, sack [gonads] and all. Damn pigs. But that is another story. Later that night the doc puts a rubber hoes [hose] on for me to pee through.

The worst part is that Miss Wolf has not noticed the difference.
I am not living happily ever after.
The End!!

REFLECTION

This version of Little Red Riding Hood is quite unique. It indicates a crude and criminal mentality. It is an orientation of the child molester. An identification with the demonic hero occurs.

Within the text itself, loss of psychological distance takes place. This happens when the wolf's den is "a trailer." Later in the story the wolf does have a den, which gives way to a trailer further on.

Punishment does happen from without, loss of penis and gonads. Yet surgery restores his ability to urinate. The "worst part" is that "Miss Wolf" didn't notice–this psychological wound.

Prison is an added punishment, but there is not mention of guilt, simply "not living happily ever after."

This fairy tale suggests the criminal mentality at its "best" (worst).

Reflecting on the fairy tales created by the prisoners, a range and depth of their stories clearly emerges with numerous themes, dynamics, and struggles–of heart and mind–and are indicated either directly or indirectly.

Bill, in the first fairy tale, introduced how the dynamics of loneliness and suicidal ideation and hopelessness are overcome by a goddess of love. Stotland (1969), in his book *The Psychology of Hope*, referring to concentration camps, states that some would give up and die due to hopelessness. In one instance, Stotland quoted from Bettelheim (1960) how hopelessness turned some into "walking corpses." Lynch (1965) has provided a terse and accurate description when he wrote that, "The sense of hope is: there is a way out. The sense of hopelessness is: there is no way out" (p. 27).

INSPIRED FICTION?: BY BILL AND TED

In Bill's case, the "hard-nose" of prison life (he had been in prison for nearly twenty years) is liveable by use of his imaginative abilities.

This is seen in his fairy tale. Brown (1975) has pointed out that the Bible itself has room for "inspired fiction or inspired narrative" (p. 100). Inspired, as used by Brown, refers to spiritual matters. Having read those comments some years ago, and now reading the prisoners' fairy tales, without stretching the idea too far, perhaps a few (say Bill's and Ted's) fairy tales might be "inspired." Inspired in no way suggests a spiritual (religious) aspect, but rather a psychological aspect. In other words, by means of personal growth (however obtained), this type of prisoner is able to write a fairy tale that not only refers to himself, but also possesses a variable of the human condition.

Secondly, a modern aspect has specifically been added to the fairy tale themes with Ted's story of addiction. So also is Bob's fairy tale regarding "The Time Machine." Perhaps this is a modern version of the Greek myths and their struggles and wishes, either in Mt. Olympus or on Earth. "The Time Machine" has the advantage of not being jealous as did Zeus and the other gods and goddesses.

Don's fairy tale is one of fighting and violence, but with the ancient purpose of being a hero. Unlike Don Quixote who rides a horse, "our Don" used a "Hog" (motorbike) and claims as his prize Snow White. Yes, the rules have changed. Tony's production of the wolf in his idea regarding "Little Red Riding Hood" portrays the criminal justifying what he wants: no holds barred. Yet, in real life, all of us are aware of the brutality of some, not all, criminals. We must keep this distinction clear.

Mike's fairy tale regarding music, but more especially dependency, introduces a theme that is everlastingly present. That theme has been voiced as the variable: we need others, but we also need to be alone. Perhaps this is a variable of the human condition we all need to do and undo, if not daily, then monthly, or for certain, yearly.

Finally, before leaving the land of fairy tales, two intriguing aspects need mentioning. In the *Velveteen Rabbit*, Williams (1981), at the end of her story, the Velveteen Rabbit becomes real–not in the boy's imagination–but really real. He then enjoys life. However, the Skin Horse remains a "real" (make believe) horse forever–and is lonely. Williams has failed to note this inconsistency. Referring to the prison population, are some prisoners "happy" to be prisoners forever: that's all they know. Whereas, the Velveteen Rabbit has a "real" life in prison, but is not "really real," so he's unhappy. Perhaps!

The Magic Flute (Die Zauberflote) was the last opera Mozart wrote.

Solomon (1995) has written an excellent summary of both the Magic Flute and of Mozart himself (pp. 505-519). In our judgement, the key concepts were argued by Solomon when he wrote, "It is profoundly troubling to be drawn by the power of music into empathic collusion with murders, tyrants, kidnappers, seducers, rapists, and misogynists" (p. 510). Further on, Solomon pointed out that Pamina near the point of suicide looks at her dagger and says, "Shalt thou then be my bridegroom?" Reflecting on that statement, Solomon wrote, "This is no idle fairy tale" (p. 513). The same can be said of the fairy tales created, from reality, by the prisoners in this chapter.

Chapter 7

STORIES FROM A BLANK PAGE

The groups progressed through a series of stages. The process began with selected Greek myths: Scott (1994) "Oedipus in Prison?" and Scott (1996) "Dionysus: Twice Born: and Criminals?" The next stage was that of reading the basic thesis (or theme) from two fairy tales: *The Velveteen Rabbit* by Williams (1981) and *The Fisherman and the Genie* recorded in Bettelheim (1976). The prisoner group members gave their reflections. The following stage consisted in having the prisoners create their own fairy tales. From their stories, six fairy tales were chosen, which were in Chapter 6.

FINAL STAGE: STORIES FROM A BLANK PAGE

The final stage consisted in having each prisoner look at a blank page and produce a story from what they were "seeing." First, however, as a "warm-up" or practice, each prisoner was asked to "make up" a story from Card B9 of the *Symonds Test* (1948). Card B9 shows an individual behind bars. Their task was to "tell a story about what you see. What's going on? What is the person thinking about? What's he feeling?" Once that task was completed, the prisoner was instructed, "Turn the card over. There is nothing on it. It is a blank page. Imagine something on it. 'See' something. Anything is okay. Tell me what you imagine or see." The following stories emerged.

STORIES

Terry

Card B9: In prison, depressed. I, uh, no money and looking for an easy way out—so he won't have to do all his time. Shame and guilt of his crime. Bar on the window—sometimes in despair, yet hopes someone will rescue me.

Blank Page: I'm walking the yard. And, I, uh, I'm realizing I forgot what the streets look like. I'm detached in the big yard. I'm walking with a few friends, but not paying attention to them. It's prison, all I know. Panic: am I institutionalized? Trying to come to grips with myself. I have three meals a day. The garden is getting pretty, I like that.

Comment: Terry's Card B9 story is a somewhat popular response—prison and depressed, yet hope of shortened time as well as guilt and shame emerge. The last sentence demonstrates loss of psychological distance when the teller of this story used "me," not "him."

His blank page story is a clear, short summary of this prisoner's lengthy stay in prison. Lost in his own thoughts, fear of institutionalization, then attempting to arrive at a realistic decision, "I have three meals a day." Then, so to speak, "Man doesn't live by bread alone," the storyteller adds, "The garden is getting pretty. I like that." This is drama of prison.

Dave

Card B9: In prison, wondering what happened to my life. Why here? I take it day by day. Look out the window and hope.

Blank page: I see, uh, reaching out, crying and still hoping for help. If someone would understand me, and listen and get things off my mind. Hoping for a friend that I can trust and open up.

Comment: In these stories we find a new prisoner seeking hope, friendship and who has a need for trust. Dave is at a low-normal intelligence and spends most of his time reaching out, using little of his own talents.

Ben

Card B9: He looks like he has no faith. Grey color. Hopeless to me. A building outside. Still glimpses of life outside.

Blank page: In my mind, another time and place. I feel like a ghost haunting myself. This goes on all the time. I feel like I'm dead. All I have is memories.

Comment: Ben provides a thematic theme of unreality. In some way it reminds me of the work of Edgar Allen Poe. One difference, Ben didn't require drugs. Prison with its concrete walls and iron ways have formed the brick walls of one of Poe's characters who wished to keep others away–built the brick walls so high he (the builder) couldn't escape.

The response to the blank page is moving–"a ghost haunting myself." This appears to be a contradiction; it is to the logical (realistic) mind. It is not to the primitive, regressed mind (unconscious?) of the dreamer. In his next effort, he attempts to be logical: "I feel I'm dead. All I have is memories." That's a sobering thought. We hear a lot about the "walking dead" and "alive corpses." Perhaps Ben has provided another avenue to be living but not alive, by only having memories.

My clinical impression of Ben is that he is quite accurate concerning how he attempts to cope with prison life.

Seth

Card B9: Abandoned by society, depressed, yet hope–the cross.

Blank Page: Out in the yard, on a bench thinking, Why do I have to go through this? Uh, I, part of life, I have to bear up.

Comment: Seth is the typical prisoner who feels sorry for himself. He's working long and hard to put himself in prison. Seth is a 46-year-old man with a teenager's romantic heart and inadequate judgement, topped and flavored with alcohol as an added ingredient. But the "dynamic catch" is that his criminal activity was all done *after he sobered up*. Seth clearly indicates the need, for him, and many other alcoholics, of a dual diagnosis which underlines the personality disorder (Axis II) as distinct from the Axis I diagnosis.

Gus

Card B9: It looks like he's enjoying the sunshine. It's a kick back day, maybe a cigarette to smoke.
Blank page: I see a clear view to the top of the mountain. A good day, it's back to nature and work.
Comment: These two stories are by Gus, who formerly wrote about being a mechanical individual. Here he's not mechanical–"he's enjoying the sunshine"–but a complete denial of reality–the iron bars. The blank page provides an opportunity to intellectualize and dream, not only for a time, but everlastingly.

Tom

Card B9: Trying to push things aside and put the attention on himself.
Blank Page: I see a lot of blackness and grey, and beyond blue clouds.
Comment: Tom is more realistic than Gus. He knows there are bars (that he's in prison) but he needs to concentrate on himself if he is going to change. The blank page is a mixture of reality (blackness) and future hope (blue clouds).

Jud

Card B9: A person in prison. A whole lot out there that he can't reach. There's a cross, so hope. He's depressed. Anyone in prison should be deep in thought. Torment, physical and emotional.
Blank Page: I want to see me in a better life. Peaceful. A happy environment. A world, a family. A step at a time. *Dr. Scott, you make me think of a lot of things.* Things that I've lost and things I regret doing. I've not lost my son, I hope (tears). I'm older in my forties. This time it hurts, but it has helped. And, uh, well I was on my way to kill a man. A car wreck. I was going to_____ . Maybe it was an outside force. I think the good Lord got angry at me–enough is enough.
Comment: Jud's stories appear realistic, seasoned with the "salt of time:" Prison keeps him from what he wants, yet the hope of the cross is encouraging. His theme on the blank page returns to religion (spiritual). He believes that "the good Lord" is fed up–and it's okay. It is,

perhaps, another way of saying that he's fed up with himself ("I'm older. . ."). If one wanted to compare, Paul was on the road to Damascus when he came to his senses. Jud was on the road "to kill a man. A car wreck." Paul was thrown from his horse. Jud needs to reflect and think. He has and he's benefitted.

Johnny

Card B9: Depressed in prison. Prison isolates us, makes us feel like freaks, that we don't fit in the outside world. I used to want people to be afraid of me.

Blank Page: Well, nothing. Well last night a dream. I've had it often. A big lake. I'm above the lake on a hill and can see an eye in the lake, just beneath the surface. (Your interpretation?) Guilty. The murder. Every day I try to keep myself busy, if not, I get screwed up. (When is a corpse not dead?) When you won't let him die in your mind. Well, I, uh, see the eye in the lake. I'm not up close to it. It's like, uh, not a monster, but something deep, scary, some heavy shit, like God. I don't want me to be known, yet, I want to talk. Doc, you came at me from a weird angle. Your talk, it's tricky. Two sides to what you say.

Comment: Johnny's response to B9 is personal. He's depressed, isolated, has fear of being a freak. Then he finally strips away the facade and his narcissistic need to have others fear and therefore not know him.

On the blank page, his immediate response is "Nothing." Following this he quickly shifts into a dream he had the previous night. In fact, it's a recurring dream. This type of dream consistently suggests a problem that is unsolved. His dream is beautifully symbolic (an eye in the lake). This he interprets (correctly) as his murder. It was a brutal murder. Earlier I had written an article entitled, "When is a Corpse Not Dead?" (Scott 1996). He supplies a correct answer, "When you won't let him die in your mind." Then he becomes vulgar ("heavy shit"), but this is his way of arriving at the goal, "like God." Now the struggle begins, "I don't want to be known" by others. Yet he has to get the guilt out. Following this, he resorts to his "style" of blaming me and my clinical technique ("your tricky style"). By this he means my effort of talking at two levels. Johnny needs to be in control, and he needs to know what's going on. My conversation places him at a disadvantage. He's aware but can't respond with certainty. In his words he calls it "two sides."

The blank page offered him an excellent opportunity (really an excuse) to utilize his need to talk about his recurring dream and to blame me. From his point of view, he is killing two birds with one stone. He thinks. Really I'm the one who is getting two birds with one tactic.

Carl

Card B9: Depressed and down on his luck. He can't do anything. I've been there. Sometimes I still am that way in my cell.
Blank Page: A group of people sitting around. Something is gone, uh, they're hurt. (What's gone?) A loved one–my murder victim.
Comment: Carl makes, shall we say, a most accurate diagnostic theme of his crime (murder) and of his DSM-IV (1994) mental health diagnostic entry.

Carey

Card B9: No idea. Behind bars. Head down, not too happy with himself.
Blank Page: I don't imagine. I did when I was a kid. (A dream?) Last night I dreamt I was in prison. Got out and came back to prison. I don't know why I came back to prison. I was disappointed to come back. I'm not going to come back in real life. (You just *imagine* you won't!) I know I'll do nothing to come back. (Your dream?) Out of the blue. I'm getting bored in prison. I'm grown up; prison is for kids.
Comment: This is the individual who has the stereotypical public, and at times prison (according to many prison officers) the profile of "a cold killer." He has been. One of the most difficult tasks is to determine if this type of prisoner is still "a cold killer." His blank page theme illustrates the struggle within regarding rehabilitation. According to his dream, he returns to prison, but not for murder. His rational (logical, awake) self is to remain out of prison, "prison is for kids." Perhaps a comparison with alcoholics would be fitting. Once an alcoholic, always an alcoholic; yet, many alcoholics remain sober. Many individuals who have committed homicide never reoffend with the same offense. The difficulty is making a correct prediction. I would agree with

Carey—I've known him for two years in group therapy.

Jeff

Card B9: A person in prison, alone. Sad, lost in his head. He is lonely and sad, thinking something he did in the past. Feels bad.

Blank page: An island. A person on it. Shipwrecked, all by himself. And, uh, no one else. He'll be saved by another ship.

Comment: Jeff's theme for card B9 is an exact picture of himself. His blank page is an ideal wish. It will not happen—he's in prison for life. In the past, he has attempted suicide. He will most likely make another attempt at suicide.

What is so significant is that two individuals commit the same crime and yet be entirely different individuals. Hence, a psychiatric/psychological diagnosis is critically needed regarding time in prison, therapy and release.

Gary

Card B9: It looks like me before my sentence. Messed up. In despair.

Blank Page: I see myself in a little room with nothing in it, only a small window. Looking out and pacing and talking to myself, "It finally happened in a mental institution." Cutting on myself. Difficult, what I see, I come close to it. I was acting out.

Comment: Gary, as was so typical of these prisoners regarding Card B9, responded with a personal theme. On the blank card he gives a history of his antics in an effort to avoid prison.

Willy

Card B9: Hiding from something. Maybe not in prison, but somewhere else in his mind. Good times, he's reliving. Trying to keep his mind off of prison.

Blank Page: Looks like a mirror of myself. I want an espresso shop. Sweat coming down my forehead. It's a nice picture.

Comment: The B9 story reflects Willy's mental condition, that of a depressive reaction (Axis I), major recurrent episodes, as well as alcoholic dependency.

Charlie

Card B9: In prison thinking of ways to get back at the people who put him in prison. He's not thinking that he put himself in prison. Bitterness inside me. And, uh, thoughts of suicide and anger and thinking back to when I was a little kid, yet hope of getting out.

Blank Page: Middle of winter. I see myself struggling with getting a positive attitude. Trying to find a job and how to get money without crime. (A year later?) Still struggling for food and lodging, but I'm working.

Comment: Once again a fairly accurate description of the storyteller. Initially, Charlie was filled with revenge. Two years of group therapy and he began to alter his decision of who really put him in prison–himself. Yet the "therapy job" is not complete, he nurses himself on his life as "a little kid."

Charlie is mature enough to provide a realistic picture on the blank page– "struggling with a positive attitude." Additionally, the "world of work" is no easy situation.

George

Card B9: Back toward window, given up hope. A lot of time to do. Escape. If not within myself and do his time.

Blank Page: I see mountains and a cabin in the valley and a lake. Smoke coming out of the fireplace, I mean, chimney. My wife coming out of front door. In my imagination hope. I've been by myself, now I need a wife.

Comment: On B9, George portrays a fairly accurate picture of himself. While on the blank page, he has added for the first time someone else, a wife. During group sessions, he constantly spoke of needing no one. The above projection indicates a major change, one he acknowledged.

Frank

Card B9: This man is locked up, looking at barred windows. Sun coming in. Wait a minute! He looks like me, a lot. Not much for him, except spiritual.

Blank Page: Act of love. He stood in front of a girl and took the rap for her. She was afraid to go to prison.

Comment: Frank has limited intellectual ability. On Card B9, he suddenly recognizes (projects) himself. The latter theme of Card B9 is carried over to the blank page in which he idealizes himself as taking "the rap" for a girl.

Red

Card B9: I see sunshine. Well, uh, thinking of freedom–but back to reality. Robbery. Wants another chance.

Blank page: Realizing who I am. I'm a human being who's facing his problems and getting out of here.

Comment: This prisoner is both intellectually and emotionally disturbed. The first variable appears in evidence, not the latter.

As the reader will observe, limited IQ produces only meager stories. As such, this technique is a poor one for this type of prisoner.

Ray

Card B9: Looks like me. Hoping to get out.

Blank Page: Illegally incarcerated. He's innocent. Shot a guy. Thinking, asking for help from the Lord.

Comment: Ray quickly identifies with the person in B9. On the blank page, he furthers that theme of being innocent. And, can we say, since he's innocent, the Lord will help him. Ray has been in and out of prison since a late teen. He is limited (low-normal) intellectually.

REFLECTIONS

Following each inmate theme, some reflections have been presented. In this final part of the chapter, some tentative and general ideas will be given.

Ben's theme to the blank page represents, it seems to me, a "stop sign." He projected himself as "a ghost (himself) haunting myself." Among the various particulars was the idea that all he has "is memories." Freud (1900) has written about "the dream's navel" (p. 525). By this notion, Freud suggested that some dreams have limitless depths.

I'd agree. Ben's thoughts suggest to me some reflections about the self as limitless horizons.

Ben's use of "a ghost haunting myself" is an application of memory. Ben had been in his group for two years. His thoughts concerning himself appear accurate. DSM-IV (1994) would label him "major depression." That label would be correct, to a point, but it would fail to touch Ben's inner self or soul. Ben is one among many prisoners who are "buried alive," more accurately, bury themselves alive and become a ghost in prison.

Maslow (1963) has suggested two types of creativity. The first type, "the creative person, in the inspirational phase of the creative furor, loses his past and his future and lives only in the moment" (p. 5), while the second type of creativity "is merely a matter of shuffling over past experiences, past habits, past knowledge to find out in what respects this current situation is similar" (p. 7).

The reader utilizing Maslow's idea of creativity will most likely "grade" the prisoner's creativity of the blank page as number two. In my judgement, Ben's story of the blank page rates a number one–truly creative. Yet, what a contradiction–he becomes a ghost to be creative!

Johnny's projection of the blank page provides for him, and for others, a rich source for self confrontation. In the past and most often in the present, Johnny's confrontation was toward others. He was too fearful (in his words, "heavy shit") to confront himself. Perhaps it is somewhat correct to think that Johnny is attempting to become creative at Maslow's second type of creativity.

Carey's challenge appears quite different. He simply believes that he will not return to prison. His dreams, however, indicated that he will return to prison. Does this pose a problem? It might. Let's assume that the reverse occurred. Carey states that he will return to prison. He will reoffend. His dream, on the contrary, would not suggest his return to prison. What parole board, if it had the power, would release him?

Any therapist working with alcoholics, other than at a superficial level, has listened to the alcoholic patient report dreams of drinking. This same alcoholic, however, remains sober. Can it be said that if an alcoholic does not dream of drinking or if the prisoner does not dream of returning to prison that repression, denial, or displacement is operative? Or is it a healthy sign not to dream of reoffending? The prison literature is nonexistent on this issue. My clinical experience of working with alcoholics is that the dream of returning to drinking affords a realistic check. More important, it provides rich clinical material.

Briefly, the themes given by the prisoners have indicated rich sources for therapeutic efforts.

Chapter 8

FOR PRISONERS: SEX IN THE KEY OF C

Sexual activity is a never-ending topic with prisoners. The ancient cliche has it: Death and taxes are certain. For the therapist working with prisoners, a new cliche is: Death, taxes—when released from prison—and sexual talk are certain. Most of the issues in this arena (sex) have not been answered. It's a safe psychological certainty they never will be answered. A "slippery slope" type of reply might be tendered by either the Supreme Court or state courts or by the people. Let's assume a hypothetical situation: the people or the state court or the Supreme Court "pass" (the people by vote, the two courts by decision) that every second female child and every third male child should be eliminated (killed, murdered) upon delivery in a given juridical district. Does this make it right? It would be legally correct. But right? What practices would emerge—have the physician hold back this fetus because it would be the third male to be born?, etc., etc.

Plato (1956) wrote *The Meno* concerning who are the teachers of virtue? He was uncertain. Apparently, the correct answer is yet awaiting discovery. MacIntyre (1984) has written an entire book concerning virtue. He pointed out that, "Emotivism is the doctrine that all evaluative judgements and more specifically all moral judgements are nothing but expressions of preference, expressions of attitude or feeling, insofar as they are moral or evaluative in character" (p. 12). Hence, it's an effort to justify what I do by not caring what you think, or if I do care, I'll persuade you to my belief.

BIBLICAL AND GILGAMESH BACKGROUND

Before addressing some sexual issues with prisoners, a most brief historical regarding sexual activity might prove interesting. In the Bible, in the book of Genesis 6:1-4, we read: "When men had begun to be plentiful on earth, and daughters had been born to them, the sons of God, looking at the daughters of men, saw they were pleasing, so they married as many as they could." The Bible (1966) commentary offers a litany of interpretation: (1) it's obscure; (2) it's a popular story from an eastern legend; (3) it's an anecdote of a race of supermen; (4) sons of God means fallen angels; and (5) sons of God were Seth's descendants, while the daughters of men were descendants of Cain (p. 21). Brown (1994), in commenting on the above passage, wrote, "Although Hebrew angelology is complex, in general, angels are regarded as males, frequently identified with 'sons of God'" (p. 300). Later in his text, Brown added, "In ancient Near Eastern and Greco-Roman polytheism, rulers, heroes, and wonder-workers were entitled 'sons of God'" (p. 480).

If we turn to Greek mythology, we learn that Dionysus was twice born. The myth stated that the goddess Hera, a sexual partner of Zeus (the chief god), became jealous of Zeus' other sexual partner, Semele. Semele was a mortal woman. Hera persuaded Zeus to appear in all his splendor to Semele. He did. The dazzling light caused Semele to abort Dionysus. Zeus, however, shall we say, lovingly took the fetus and sewed it (Dionysus) in his thigh. In due time, Dionysus was born. Here we encounter by means of a Greek myth the coupling of a god (Zeus) with a mortal woman (Semele).

Gilgamesh, as translated by Mason (1970), has offered a unique theme regarding sexual intercourse. *Gilgamesh* is an ancient story. Some authors hold that it is older than the Bible. Gilgamesh, an ancient king, had everything that he wanted, except everlasting life. He undertook a journey to find everlasting life. In his journey, he encountered Enkidu. Enkidu was like an animal covered with hair and ran "like a gazelle." Enkidu became human. This transformation occurred following intercourse with a woman. In the words of the story, "One morning she awoke him and said to him, Why do you want to run with the animals? You are a human being now, not like them" (p. 20). What a beautiful story. It does appear that "making love," not making sex, does have the innate potential to make one truly human. We ask the question: What is the typical phenomenon today?

In all group therapy, discussion of sexual matters arises. Depending on the composition and location, this topic receives considerable attention. My experience of working with prisoners has indicated that length of confinement tends to foster sexual discussion.

Scott (1977), in his article, "The Sexual Offender," covered a wide range of sexual activity regarding offenders: child molestation, rape, incest, and female exhibitionists. This latter section of the article related some typical behavior of female ex-prisoners. Behavior of one woman included that she "would unbutton her blouse, pull out a breast and dunk it in someone's beer" at the tavern (p. 256).

Sex, as it emerges in group therapy, provides a variety of avenues: to brag, to put down the opposite sex, to foster vulgar talk sprinkled with anger and outbursts of emotions. Fantasy is a dominant variable for many, if not most, sex offenders. In the chapter on treatment (Chapter 10), we will offer some suggestions regarding this difficult clinical issue. From the sex offender's point of view, the reader can refer to Appendix II. Although group therapy is a place for the expression of emotions, some structure is required or group "therapy" quickly regresses to an "id orgy" of expression.

Occasionally a prisoner attempts to stamp out all emotional involvement with sexual activity, even to avoid sex completely. The following is one such effort. It is Gus's attempt to intellectualize the problem:

> To raise your voice in anger is to break a prison rule. To whistle is to break a rule. This means we can't enjoy emotion in action. The rules say I'm responsible for all that I do. To express emotions is illegal. I've spent years paying for my last emotional burst–killing a female, about sex. So I'll have to get rid of the sexual emotions. I can handle a lot of other pressure, but not the sexual stuff. So I'll be neutral. On the outs, there's no room for emotions, sexual ones.
>
> You might ask, where does this mechanical passion come from? Simply this: acting on emotion is what my crime was about. I don't want to do it again, so I am eliminated all factors that led to it. Much like an ex-alcoholic: to give up drinking requires resisting a whole lot of desires that in themselves may not be bad, but will lead to drinking.
>
> I've never been proud of my sexuality. It has not caused a single thing to my benefit or liking. If I don't benefit, why have it? No one has yet proved me wrong, neither any of the group members nor you, Dr. Scott.

In reply, this prisoner would never experience any emotion in group sessions. He chose and remained a student of the group sessions. He wouldn't get his "emotions dirty with an experience." He typifies the individual who can pass a written test but flunk all the clinical classes. The careful reader will have caught the phrase "mechanical passion," a contradiction. Several times in group he either would not participate in psychodrama, or on those instances when he did, he would "pull out" as the emotional material emerged.

At times, some very sensitive material arose around child molestation. The issue was "What do you do with the child?" We had sessions regarding empathy. We handed out questionnaires. Some of the child molesters appeared to benefit from group. Yet the following erupted to an outburst of expression:

Charlie: Kill the victim. I wished I had been killed twenty years ago when I was raped. When I get on alcohol, I've tried to kill myself. What a woman must go through when she's raped!

Dr. Scott: If you raped a woman, would you kill her?

Dennis: Not me.

Charlie: Well, uh, no, I guess.

Ray: Not me. I was raped as a kid.

Mark: That's not easy to decide. That last part, my victim said as I stabbed her, "Don't." I didn't stop.

Irwin: I was molested as a kid. I'm darn glad I wasn't killed. I'm doing okay. Charlie, what the hell is wrong with you?

Charlie: That's the way I feel.

Irwin: To hell with your feelings—don't put them on others. If you feel so bad, why don't you kill yourself and not just try?

Dennis: Yeah, that's what I say.

From this short dialogue, one grasps the range of beliefs and reaction to sexual crime—or being the victim of a sexual crime. Charlie was one of my most disturbed, confused and complex cases. It's my opinion that not only the crime but especially a thorough and accurate psychological examination of the criminal is crucial regarding length and type of treatment.

THREE DRAWINGS BY THE SAME PRISONER

Though prisoners benefit from their ability to express their inner selves, and conflicts, treatment benefits at times by artistic efforts. From the many drawings I have received, I have selected the artistic work of one prisoner.

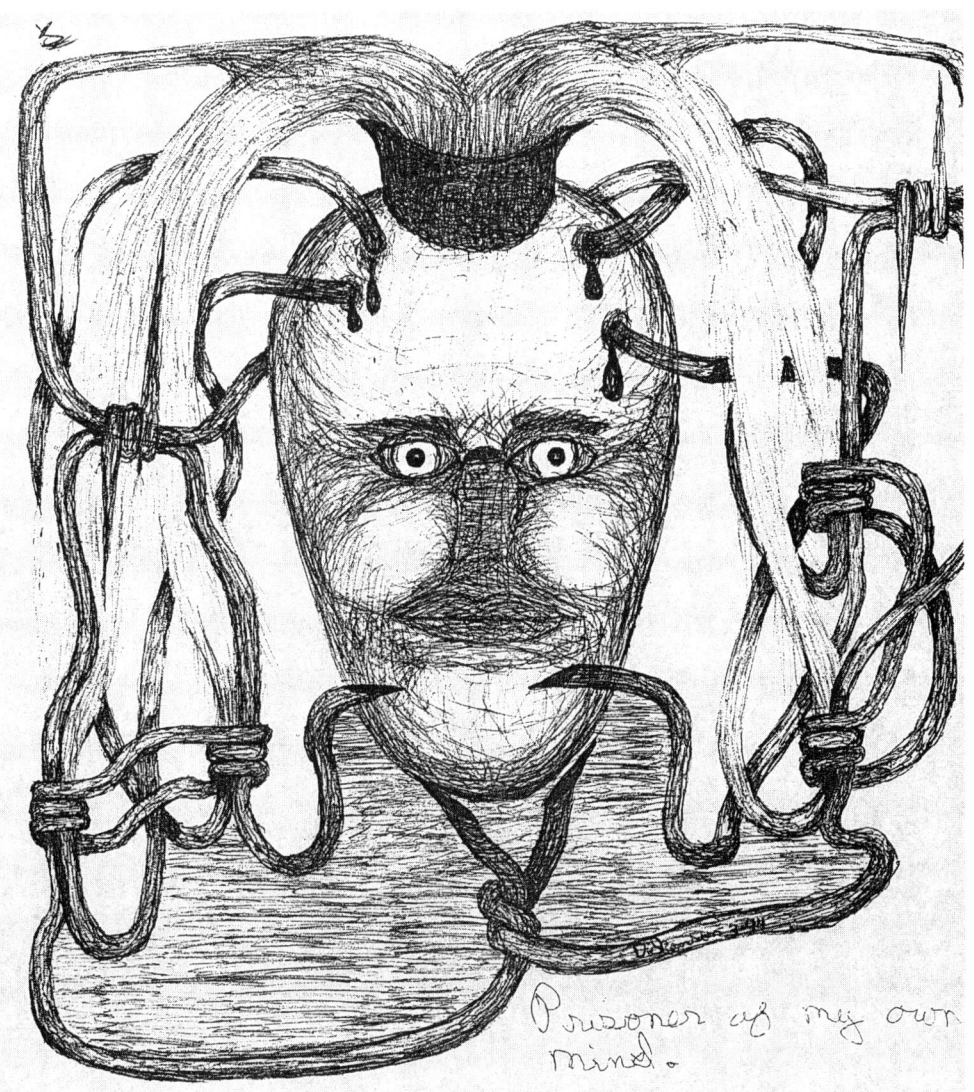

Figure 2. The "Mind of the Prisoner: illustrates his confusion.

This represents, as he entitled this drawing, "Prisoner of My Own Mind." Following this drawing, prisoner Tom began to release emotions and thoughts that he had harbored for years. In group therapy, he stated, "This is the first time I've been encouraged to draw what's inside me."

Figure 3. "Crucified To My Sexual Problems." A symbolic illustration of the same prisoner's struggle with his sexual problems.

Figure 3 represents how he is tied (crucified) to his sexual problems. During group, prisoner Tom said, "It's hard to look at myself. It hurts. It scares me. (Tears.) Lately, something inside says, 'Why change?'" It was pointed out that he stopped alcohol (he is an alcoholic) before coming to prison. His reply was, "Alcohol is more physical than mental, the headache . . . sex is really more mental."

In Figure 4 prisoner Tom printed out (top left) that "It's me. I'm wanting to kill. I don't care about my victim," while at the top right, "It's a hole in the wall. If I don't change, I'll be in prison until the wall falls in. The flowers (roses in center) are the good things in life that turn into something bad. The mountain cabin (right lower side) is where I could live and not get into trouble. At the bottom (three small roses) is death—I can't change my thinking."

It's my opinion that these drawings, and others, were an avenue for therapeutic changes.

WHAT DO YOU KNOW ABOUT THE MOMENT/TIME OF YOUR CONCEPTION?

Some years prior to working in prison, I had conducted group therapy for delinquent girls housed in an institution. They had been around the block, sexually, several times. Sexual issues emerged often during the group sessions. Typically, giggling, Shakespearean asides, brass and bravado statements were dispersed during these periods. In my clinical opinion, little, if any, therapeutic benefits resulted. After some thought on the problem, the girls were asked, "What do you know about the moment or the time your mother conceived you?" It was one of the most productive sessions we had. The theme lingered on for many sessions. Some of the girls recalled (emotionally) the time/moment of conception for their own children. Tears, anger, depression, regret, and hatred were the usual responses. Based in part on the above clinical experience, three prisoner therapy groups were asked: What do you know about the moment/time of your conception? Many of the members did not know the word conception. It was explained.

Figure 4. "Inner Turmoil and Stages." Stages in his treatment effort regarding his sexual problems.

Group 1

Harry: I'm the result of a leaky rubber. I've heard it...it devalues me.

Seth: My parents were going to marry. My mom got PG in the back seat of a car. I wanted to know. I thought I was adopted.

Ben: Mom doesn't know if it was my dad or a boyfriend. She was an easy ride. What I've heard, he got her drunk...

Jim: Too hard to talk about. I can't, well, uh, my dad was 17 and Mom was 12 years older...

Dave: Two stories. It hurts, being lied to, not wanted or an accident.

Harry: Mom wanted a girl.

Ben: I'm sorry I said Mom was an easy ride.

Dr. Scott: Harry, do you wish the rubber hadn't broken?

Harry: Yeah, well, yeah...I have a child but didn't plan on it. (This was followed with considerable emotions by Harry. This information furnished the discussion for the remainder of the session as well as following sessions.)

Group 2

Joe: I was planned, but they never thought I'd be in prison.

Sam: I was planned, loved for a time. Now they don't care.

Dick: My mom sees me as a failure. She had to marry Dad.

Ron: I won't talk about it. (Turns away in anger.)

Tom: My parents talk about it a lot. I was planned. I don't know the time I was conceived.

Mike: My mother was insane. When I was born she said, "Go." (Mike rambled on in what appeared to be psychotic talk and had to be quieted.)

Joe: I've thought of not being born many times. It's a humiliating journey, prison...

Albert: I never knew my dad. Mom wouldn't tell me. I was conceived in a brown house in Arkansas. He wanted sex. Mom was twenty years younger. I think, uh,...I'd kill him. (Cries. Can't talk for a bit.) I've been a failure. (Cries.)

Group 3

Pete: I'm not sure my parents loved each other, but the relationship was rocky. I, uh, once mom was PG, I was wanted. I don't know about before she was PG.

Phil: A sick thought. It's dirty. It's sick. You're sick.

Mickey: Probably both my parents were drunk. I was not wanted. I was told this many times. I had fetal alcohol syndrome. I wished I was not born. I don't like being here. I have a daughter, me and my girlfriend. Both of us was drunk. I don't regret my kids, but their mother, she was a no good bitch . . .

Dale: That question, dirty. I won't answer it–to think of my parents having sex.

Jack: I can't imagine it. Never thought of it. (Think of it now.) No–its something not supposed to think of.

Pete: I suppose it's taboo.

Ralph: I can't imagine it–sex between parents, I, no.

Phil: It's sick.

Dale: I'm upset with you.

Phil: Sex is serious business. May cost your life–diseases.

Pete: Phil, you're insecure. I used to let my penis talk for me. (Pete then added that once after sex with a pick-up woman, she asked, "Shit on me. I feel so shitty of what I've done." This disclosure prompted an energetic discussion, not only at this session, but the following week.)

Mac: The question is tough. How do *you* come up with this stuff? I can't answer it.

REFLECTIONS

In Group 3, both Phil and Dale were convicted of homicide. The latter was a rape-murder conviction. Phil was also in prison for murder. What a reaction they present–shocked that such a "dirty question" (Tell us about the moment you were conceived.) was asked! They then regress to the "old trick" of argumentum ad hominem–attacking my personality: "You're sick." Phil does "sober up" for a few moments and reflects on his own sexual activity–"Sex is serious business. May cost your life–diseases." Ralph presented himself as a "saintly" paranoid: "I can't imagine it." In my experience he imagined a lot of things about others, but his halo was always shining.

Jack instantaneously makes up his own "hide-saving rules" (i.e., "...it's something not supposed to think of").

Pete, the "hero" of the discussion, first speculated on the relationship of his parents ("it was rocky"), but "once Mom was PG, I was wanted." Eventually he turns to his own sexual activity saying, "I used to let my penis talk for me." Then added the request by one of his sexual partners as indicated above. Mickey became involved in that discussion. After calling his wife a "no good bitch," spoke of suicidal thoughts.

In Group 1, Harry spoke of the "leaky rubber" when he was conceived. That his parents shared this with Harry is a classical case of rejection and passive aggression. In spite of the above, Harry relates that he has a child he didn't plan on. According to Harry, he did not share this with his child. Harry expresses a wish that his parents hadn't used a "leaky rubber."

For the majority of the other members, the question resulted in difficulty–lack of knowledge regarding whom the real father was and out and out hurt.

Regarding Group 2, there is a wide range from "I was planned" to "My mother was insane." Sandwiched in between was the statement of Albert, "I'd kill him," referring to his father. Joe provides a note that his being in prison is "humiliating for my parents."

The above discussion forged the title for this chapter, "Sex in the Key of C." "C" means conception. The prisoners' reaction to this question provoked an extremely wide range of emotions and thoughts. Two homicide prisoners (one associated with rape) termed the question "dirty" and attacked me. Now, that's "emotional life" (from the heart?) at its best high note–in the key of C? Others wished they had not been born. Pete (whom I termed the "hero") revealed what a "pick-up" woman asked him to do ("Shit on me.") Finally, a few members related the moment of conception for their own children.

The concept of a "leaky rubber" was, it seemed, a difficult reflection for most of these "hardened" prisoners.

We will conclude this chapter with the thoughts of Joey regarding fantasy and sex, which appear in Appendix II.

Chapter 9

GROUP PSYCHOTHERAPY

INTRODUCTION

Plato (1956) in his *Symposium* believed that a philosopher was halfway between a sage and a fool. Perhaps this idea can be applied to the group therapist working with prisoners. Some—maybe the majority—would suggest that the group therapist of prisoners would be closer to being a "therapeutic fool." The etymology of philosopher is a lover of wisdom, not a wise person. This orientation holds, also, for the group therapist with prisoners—he wants (wishes, expects) that the prisoner becomes a better (a more mature) individual.

Recently, health organizations have indicated that the focus be directed away from infectious problems. Rather, the focus suggested was to be on the chronic diseases: heart, cancer, and depression. The latter is a mental disorder (disease). I want to add to the above list, *crime*! Numerous authorities complain that therapy has not been successful. It has been suggested that "a quick-fix" or a "Band-Aid" or a series of lectures should be sufficient. If crime can be likened to a chronic disease, and I believe it can, a more realistic approach is required.

Scott (1973) published a book relating his experience of working with prisoners in prison, and later these same individuals when on parole. A life style change was difficult. Prison was a known factor, while the "streets" were less stable, more unpredictable, work was not that rewarding, and "the call for excitement" (i.e., another crime) was addictive-like. The "fast buck" was ever knocking for attention. It is with certitude that we can say that not everyone who leaves the hospital is cured; rather, a continuation of meds, follow-up exams, or if a chronic condition has been diagnosed, life-long medical attention continue. The same, we believe, holds true regarding prisoners leaving prison. In fact, in a former chapter, the prisoners themselves voiced the need for follow-up treatment. It has been found that having the prisoner do the PET provides, typically, a method of risk dynamics. This can be utilized in group as certain topics emerge.

A POLYSEMOUS THESIS

The final comment in this introductory note makes reference to a polysemous thesis. Hatcher (1990) has provided an excellent review and offered illustrations for this idea. The outstanding illustration of this idea was given by Dante. This illustrates a theological orientation. Hatcher has utilized the basic polysemous idea by using a psychological example: that of a cigar. The basic idea remains whether working with a theological or a psychological orientation, Hatcher has insisted. She illustrates by a cigar: (1) historical: refers to past use; (2) moral: that "a cigar is symptomatic of a present psychological state, be it an oral craving . . . or aggressive desire to harass other people" (p. 355); or (3) anagogical: "Smokers may pay for their habit with their lives" (p. 355). Basically then, "a psychological core meaning may be seen in the theme of oral cravings" (p. 355), referring to past, present, or future impact of cigar smoking.

Can the prisoner be viewed in a polysemous sense? If so, what are the advantages, if any? Or is society and the prisoner better viewed in the literal sense: a prisoner is just a prisoner? A cigar can be viewed as just a cigar. Hatcher argued–or shall we say, pointed out–"The decay of the polysemous approach also made rise of the experimental science" (p. 365).

Is there any significant difference in these two examples: a cigar vs. a prisoner? Lately, the turmoil clearly indicates the underlining of the anagogical sense regarding smoking. Is society concerned for itself or for the prisoner? Each of us has our own reply.

In a polysemous approach, the prisoner (offender) can be viewed from the "eternal" history of crime–forever in the past. In the moral (present and psychological) sense, crime reflects the psychological presence (state) of an id orientation. By this we mean greed or anger, acting out and acting up, sex, etc. as well as the ego state of belief in being some kind of victim–genetic (ADHD, alcoholism, depression), family (dysfunction), and poor environment.

What about the anagogical sense? Texts have been penned in this area: rehabilitation, or simply punishment. Yet, large segments of society express fear of criminals. Some segments of law enforcement champion, "Three strikes and you're out." Other segments—or are they the same segments?—of society have mantras: "Who knows what is right and wrong?;" "If it feels good, do it;" etc., etc. My own thesis is: the criminal loses in the very area he most prizes: freedom. He is either "watched" by a PO or is in prison. What is required is a change in the moral (present and anagogical) state, namely a maturing of the individual offender. It is my belief, based on experience, that for some offenders, treatment helps by assisting this change to occur.

The reader will have noted in the previous chapters techniques, procedures, and ideas utilized effectively with prisoners in group therapy. The remainder of this chapter suggests a somewhat formal orientation based on years of experience with prisoners in prison and offenders on parole.

SOME HISTORICAL NOTES REGARDING GROUP PSYCHOTHERAPY

The majority of my clinical experience, over twenty years of working with offenders either in prison or on parole, has been group therapy. What model, what structure, or technique does one use with this type of individual?

Dies (1992), in a survey, asked "senior clinicians with the American Group Psychotherapy Association to identify the major orientation" (p. 2). Ten models were identified. Analyzing the data, Dies believed that three major groups could be clearly noted: psychodynamic, interpersonal, and action-oriented. He further found "91 percent of the action-oriented therapists value cognitive reframing, which is judged to be important by only 13 percent of the interpersonal and by 6 percent of the psychodynamic practitioners" (p 13).

In a prison system, officials want action-oriented (don't act up or act out). My personal preference is that of attitude change, that is a change of mind and heart. This can be framed, briefly, by a change from a paranoid orientation to that of *met anoia*. The Greek etymology for paranoia is: *para* (twisted) and *noia* (think); whereas, for *met anoia* it is: *meta* (to cross) and *noia* (think). Hence, to change one's mind, or change one's style, or to change one's direction. It appears that *met anoia* can be linked with anagogical.

If the previous terminology is too involved with Greek, Frank's (1973) assumptive world has given this basic concept another point of view. In his thesis, Frank has postulated that all of us in order to have some "order and regularity on the welter of experiences impinging upon him" (p. 27), have a set of assumptions. Some of these assumptions come from early life, some later. Some are difficult for the individual to change while other assumptions are readily altered. According to Frank, an assumption has cognitive, emotional, and behavioral aspects. The cognitive aspect is the assigning of a cause to an event. But assigning a cause is heavily influenced by emotional elements. One's anger, jealousy, etc. influence the emotional element. Behavior–what one does–rounds out an assumption. Our totality of assumptions is our "assumptive world." Change requires altering one's assumptions. Therapy has the difficult but important part in helping the individual (in the present instance, the prisoner) in changing his assumptions.

According to the present author's knowledge, none of the senior clinicians surveyed by Dies had conducted group therapy in prison. In fact, only lately has the American Group Psychotherapy Association included prison group therapy in its annual meetings. In the 1996 meeting on February 15, a session entitled "Group Therapy for Incarcerated Youths and Adults" was held. Dr. Campos spoke regarding the incarcerated youth. Scott presented a talk entitled, "Group Work With Disturbed Offenders in a State Prison."

An attempt is now made to present what we might call "the atmosphere" for group therapy with offenders.

MY PRISONER GROUPS' REACTIONS TO ZIMBARDO'S SIMULATION OF PRISON

In the early 1970s, my groups (Scott, 1973) (in prison and those on parole) listened to a tape concerning Zimbardo's simulation of prison interaction between inmates and guards. Stanford students were selected to be either inmates or guards. In brief, the "study" had to be stopped. Things got out of control. My group members laughed and commented:

1. "If we cried or got upset we'd get out of group?"
2. "Let's get emotional, and they'd let us out of prison."
3. "What a bunch of babies."
4. Etc., etc.

Sleek (1996) has written a summary of Zimbardo's experiment on its twenty-fifth anniversary. The author noted that recently this research was viewed over "60 Minutes" on CBS. During the 1996 review, Zimbardo remarked that his girlfriend (now his wife) became upset at viewing the action. The experiment was halted. Among the various conclusions, Zimbardo believed that a unique and untypical experience can have a detrimental effect on a person. If so, one wonders what the typical response would have occurred if prisoners suddenly found themselves in a Stanford (or other university) classroom and had to pass!

One of the lessons to be learned is that some type of structure is required for unique experiences. My basic structure request for the prison group (and all groups) is: "Talk it out; don't act it out." This basic structure favors both the prison administration (don't act it out) and the therapist (talk it out). The "Father" of group therapy, Slavson (1964), has underlined the above in his writings. Slavson appeared to grasp the essence of this concept when he wrote, "Acting-out by adults is always a sign of regression and a weak ego" (p. 378). The concept is easy to grasp. Its successful application is more difficult. Anyone associated with offenders knows that talking all too frequently leads to arguments which often leads to action: hitting, striking, hurting. An important distinction made by Fine (1973) is that poor impulse control is often ego-dystonic, while acting-out is ego-syntonic. An important therapist role is to formulate that distinction as the individual prisoner begins to spin out his story and to watch his interaction with other group members. This book has provided examples of ego-dystonic and ego-syntonic orientation.

BASIC GROUP PSYCHOTHERAPY ORGANIZATION, TECHNIQUES, AND EXAMPLES OF CLINICAL MATERIAL

I have learned through years of experience in state hospitals, juvenile detention homes, and outpatient work with alcoholics and drug dependency individuals to select members for various groups. Alcoholics taught me this lesson. Just because an individual is an alcoholic, little else may be in common. Compare, for instance, an antisocial alcoholic with a dystonic (depressive) alcoholic. What is significant is not the alcoholism but the type of individual who has the alcoholism. As a result, the alcoholic clinic had a variety of groups, although all were alcoholic. So, also, with prisoners. Typically my prison groups are divided into groups of:

1. Low functioning and chronic: low IQ, little drive to succeed
2. Tough guys: angry, know-it-alls, like to run everything
3. Emotional: easily upset, suicidal or a least parasuicidal, small in stature, dystonic for their crime
4. Sexual: rapists, child molestation, other sexual problems
5. Best group: can observe the self, short period of crime, psychologically minded, and advanced defense mechanisms.

Obviously, different techniques are required. I will offer but a few examples: for group number one (low functioning) there is more support but not so for group number two. Rationalizations are least tolerated for the sexual group, while insight is fostered for group number five.

Yet with all these different types of prison groups is there a common procedure? I believe so, namely, "Put yourself under observation, not someone else." These prisoners believe they have 20-20 vision about everyone, even the low functioning and for certain the tough guys groups. The prisoner or any other individual is still in the first phase of treatment as long as he continues to look at others. This is where the task of the group therapist is most difficult, namely, *you* observe him, since he can't do it himself. This technique is done not simply as a "put-down," but rather an effort to "coach" him in the progress. This process is preferable, but more explosive, when another member of the group makes an observation of a member. The following is an example:

Larry:	Yesterday I was trying, well, at supper time, Ben was sitting by himself. I looked at him.
Ben:	Larry, why in hell were you looking at me?
Larry:	I was joking around. Then something kicked in. When you asked, "What the hell you looking at?" We both have anger problem. Bad!
Fred:	Started as a joke?
Ben:	(directly to Larry) Larry, what's your problem?
Larry:	Joking with you. I'm, uh, well, sorry.
Ben:	(hesitates a bit): I'll accept your apologies. I'm trying to control my anger.
Larry:	Well, I was, uh, well, a hypocrite. The other night I was telling someone not to pester this other prisoner.
Ben:	We were in the rec room and you said you wanted to give me a karate chop.
Larry:	I was joking.
Tom:	Jokes or threats?
Larry:	I see Ben alone and I want a conversation.
Ben:	What's there to talk about?
Larry:	All kinds of stuff.

This might appear trivial to the outsider. In prison, the above could set off a fight. Both Ben and Larry are quick to anger and both are somewhat low functioning. The above dialogue is a success for them.

The second example is that of two tough guys, both in for murder.

Joe:	My relationship with peers is poor.
Dr. Scott:	I observe you in group as always having to be right.
Joe:	Well, Greg and I were, well, we blew up. We got over it. We talked.
Greg:	It was touchy for a time.
Dr. Scott:	You two, you know that one of the major goals in group is to "talk it out." So I want to congratulate you two.
Joe:	Thanks, Dr. Scott.
Greg:	Thanks, Dr. Scott.

This bit of an episode provides what can be done. Moreover, it is not unique. Azar (1994) has written, "Cognitive therapy, group therapy, behavioral therapy, psychoanalysis–they all work to help people deal with emotional stress. But why do they all work? One common denominator is disclosure: the telling of one's story" (p. 22). This notion was stressed in the opening chapter in this book. We noted at that time that for prisoners, two factors require attention: the story must be the prisoner's story, not someone else's story, and one must be alert to the story within the story.

Over the years, I've assumed methods of speaking with the group members. A given is that in prison life the officer is never wrong. I've observed this phenomenon on the ward or in staff sessions. Hence, in group I state, "You can disagree with me, and I can disagree with you. We can make this exchange, for the most part, with some maturity. Yelling, shouting, and swearing will not be permitted." Some have difficulty with this freedom and seem to merely enjoy opposing me. I bring this to their attention at times. I challenge them to have "deeper and better thoughts," saying, "You think a mile long and an inch deep."

In most instances, a type of free exchange develops. Often humor emerges. Humor has many sides. In prison, it is often sarcastic, belittling, getting even, challenging, and dirty. "Good" humor is fostered. Examples are seeing that there is another side to the situation, and not being so defensive or heavy or paranoid. For the most part, humor and freedom to disagree among each other and with the therapist has the effect of a healthy aura.

Misunderstandings do occur. Each member of the group has his own two ears. He might choose only what appears to satisfy his wishes. Another member only seemingly listens with his "bad" ear, hearing only negative things. The list is endless. If one member (a quiet one) is urged to speak, the "mouthy" member feels put down when he's asked to listen. In our thesis, the entire prison is a giant, tangled, sibling struggle. Group is caught up in this web. Group, however, has an opportunity to work at this important issue.

One of the group approaches which I've found to be difficult, if not impossible, is that of "technical neutrality." This means that the therapist is equi-distant from id, ego, and superego factors. Even when certain group members were given the opportunity to be the leader with a technical neutrality approach, it failed. An example, Bill was the leader; within five minutes he stated, "This pisses me off."

SOME ADVANCED GROUP PSYCHOTHERAPY TECHNIQUES AND ORIENTATION

As mentioned throughout this book, techniques and procedures can't be "simply slapped" on group members. This applies in a special way to prisoners. Earlier, I (Scott, 1973) reported my failure of attempting hypnosis with prisoners too early in group. Later, with the same group, hypnosis was effective. With the above in mind, some specific techniques are indicated.

Suicide Note

A particular prisoner had written a suicide note. He was referred to group. During group therapy, he was asked "to write a suicide note." He was given a pencil and a piece of paper for the task. Resistance arose at once. A bargaining process began. He'd write the suicide note if, after showing it, he could immediately tear it up. Once written, he tore it up saying, ". . . it could be used against me." This was an object lesson, if not for this particular patient, for the other group members. It was a type of psychodrama.

A Dream Task

A prisoner had never visited his wife's grave. He was asked, "Dream of your wife." At the next session the following week, to his surprise, he did dream. In his words, "I went to her grave. We had a talk. She asked me about my crimes. I told and also said that I still loved her. A big part of me died with her. Well, uh, I uh, on the ward I play the Village Idiot. I can't face painful things."

The Diaper

A prisoner in his late twenties (Johnny) who had the maturity of a child–angry, attention seeking, crying, nothing was his fault–was eventually directed to "put on a diaper." A piece of paper from a hand towel machine was given to him. At once he became angry–*he had a temper tantrum*. The group, an "advanced" group, agreed that he should take the paper towel, put it on his lap indicating that it was a diaper. One member disagreed. Johnny was asked, "Do you want to put it on yourself or Bill?" Johnny put it on himself. He sat, "diaper on," said nothing for some moments, then said, "Yeah, I'm immature." The following week Johnny remarked regarding the profound effect "putting on the diaper had on me."

One month later he was transferred to another facility. Three months following his transfer, Johnny wrote me a letter. In the letter, Johnny wrote, "Yes, the diaper episode did help me a lot in that I realized that I am an immature kid (baby) when I don't get my way. That's my belief, that as long as I want to grow, I will."

SYMBOLISM AND REALITY

A tough, angry prisoner, one with a limited vocabulary, when he did attempt to (finally) express an opinion about himself stated, "I'm a piece of shit." This occurred during an evaluation meeting. It occurred to me that somehow this statement should be utilized. He was asked to have a bowel movement and bring it to group. His anger flared. My response was, "Think about it." Next group session I noted, "Sam, you didn't do what was asked. If you can't, will you at least tell the group what was asked of you?" He refused. This continued for five sessions.

At the sixth session, Sam said, "Dr. Scott, you, uh, well, had wanted me to do something, my past feelings about myself. When I said 'I feel like a piece of shit,' you wanted me to shit on a piece of paper and bring it to group. Damn it, in the past I've thrown shit on the staff and had no remorse. Now I do. Weird, man, weird."

Jeff: Yeah, I knew of what you did.
Sam: Dr. Scott, you, well, when I said I feel like a piece of shit I meant I felt like a freak.
Jerry: I think Dr. Scott's request was reasonable. He gets to the point. Dr. Scott is breaking your convict wall.
Sam: He's not.
Jerry: He is.
Jake: At one time, I didn't give a shit about myself. Not now. I can talk. Group has helped.
Jerry: Yeah. I see that.

Dr. Scott:	Jake, you kept talking about being a stand-up man. Well, finally you're standing up to yourself. Sam, you've begun the process.
Jake:	Yeah, but it's hard.
Jerry:	Don't snivel. Now, you have a start.
Jim:	I'm new to the group. I'm trying to stand up to my own stuff.

REFLECTION

All of the above "dynamic group events" were effective in a variety of ways. The suicide note episode was instructive for the other group members, but not for the author of the note. In example two, this appeared to be an "easy" response–the dream. It presented to the prisoner to get beyond his conscious defenses. The diaper (the third example) was given considerable thought. He had been in prison, left, and returned. Obviously, something dramatic was indicated. The diaper came to mind. The effectiveness appears confirmatory by the prisoner's letter months after leaving group and being transferred to another facility.

Example four is clearly the most difficult and, to a certain extent, risky. What helped to promote my decision was the idea that I could depend for support from Jake and Jerry. Jake had previously used the phrase "I'm a piece of shit," but was gradually changing. Jerry, from past experience was the most psychologically minded in group and strong enough to say exactly what he felt.

The following is not a technique but emerged out of group therapy sessions. The prisoner voiced doubts if he wanted to know who he was. Incidentally, he lacked the drive (or destiny) of Oedipus, who wanted to know who he was (Scott, 1994). The present prisoner patient (Herb) stated, "I'd be better off not knowing. I'd be worse off knowing. I'm not who I think I am."

Dr. Scott:	Will you dream about it?
Herb:	It's always a nightmare... I'm tied down and big rats bite me. I, uh, think of suicide; that would make it even...

ARTWORK

Eventually, Herb brought the following art work to group.

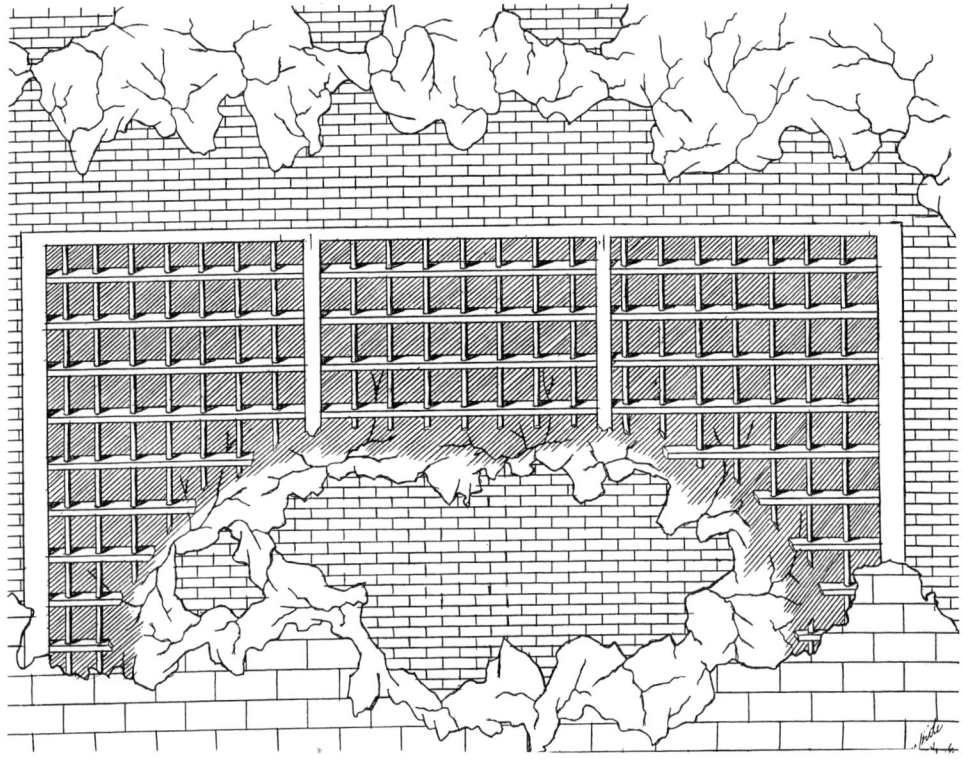

Figure 5. "The Wall I've Built Around Myself." The prisoner's effort to "wall himself in," which he now realizes he needs to break through.

Herb's explanation was:
1. The door means going into either my heart or my head.
2. With my head, the drawing is about my past. The circles and troubles getting bigger, from bottom to top.
3. The wall represents what I built around me. I'm, uh, I'm getting out through the door.
4. He was asked, "Are you going to leave the wall down?" Herb replied, "I have to get self-esteem back. Before I didn't care, just wrapped up in myself."

We have termed what Herb stated "just wrapped up in myself" as navel gazing. This is not unique with Herb. The reader will have gleaned the two extremes: (1) always looking at and judging someone else; or (2) "eternally" preoccupied with the self. It is a difficult treatment task to have "one eye on the self and one eye on reality."

At times prisoners appear to absorb the impact of treatment. There is a need to express what they are undergoing. The following is an example.

Figure 6. "Struggles Within Myself." An attempt to illustrate the progress a prisoner has made (white); yet he still has significant problems which remain (dark).

This prisoner's drawing portrays his progress in treatment as represented by the white part of the figure; the black portion indicates that he still needs to make further progress, to tame his anger, hostility, and at times rage. Ellenberger (1970) has given attention to the idea of "creative illness." It appears, to a degree, that this is an example of "convict creative illness."

TRUE PLAY AND PLAYFULNESS LACKING IN PRISONERS

I have left the most difficult variable of group therapy to the last: play. Play and playfulness are natural and easy, but not for prisoners. Previously, we had written on humor. Most authorities regarding ego defenses place humor at the top of the list. Freud (1974) insisted that humor is "among the great series of methods which the human mind has constructed in order to evade the compulsion to suffer" (p. 163). Frequently, what prisoners regard as humor is either making fun of someone, sarcasm, or sexual (which is down and dirty).

I first attempted playfulness when I worked in a juvenile detention home for boys, age 15 to 18 years of age. My peers and supervisor were quite skeptical. They told me that playfulness would confuse my role. My response was that fathers have a variety of roles: teacher, confidant, providing for the family, and playful; in short, a well-rounded model. Initially, I began what might not appear as playful. These delinquent teenaged boys had to listen to two hours of classical music once a week. They were told, "I listen to your stuff the rest of the week." Good-natured joking and playfulness emerged. For their turn, they sat me down to listen to "real music." Ugh!

From the above, weight lifting, basketball, and conversation took on a new meaning. In brief, the roles became more natural. For some of the boys, it was their first "natural" father.

Later, when I began working with alcoholics and their spouses, a naturalness was fostered. Scott (1989) reported on humor and play with alcoholics. The alcoholics in the sample were 80 males and 40 females. In response to one question, they judged that alcoholics have less humor than others. This was especially true of female alcoholics. It was found that "94 percent of the male respondents and 95 percent of the female respondents believe that humor in treatment is useful" (p. 34).

Beyond humor is, I believe, play and playfulness. In group therapy for alcoholics; an attempt was made to have sessions similar to being in the tavern—without alcohol. This was a difficult task. Why? Because the typical alcoholic is often not humorous without alcohol and certainly not playful.

Play/playfulness in prison group therapy? This author is not aware of any professional literature on this topic. I've learned that prisoners on parole tend to be more playful than those in prison. Prisoners make crude attempts at play. We would term their efforts to be "horsing around without horse sense."

Before proceeding, what is meant by the term play? We know of no better description than that given by Anthony and Winnicott. Winnicott (1968) wrote, "Where playing is not possible then the work done by the therapist is directed towards bringing the patient from a state of not being able to play into a state of being able to play" (p. 591). Although Winnicott was a child psychiatrist, he insisted, "Whatever I say about children playing really applies to adults as well" (p. 592). On reflection, Winnicott said, "As I look back over the papers that mark the development of my own thought and understanding I can see that my present interest in play is the relationship of trust" (p. 596).

Anthony (1968) gave the lecture celebrating 25 years of group psychotherapy. Incidently, I was fortunate to be present. Toward the end of his lecture, Anthony argued, "Play is self-creation, and play, for me at least, is therapy and therapy is play. It is my belief that people come to us depressed, deadened, defeated, and destroyed in order to be set free to play" (p. 299). Shortly, he added, "So many adults that I meet, even therapists, do not seem to have had a childhood and consequently have little notion of play in this self-creative sense" (p. 299).

G.K. Chesterton (1950) has argued that *A Midsummer Night's Dream* is greater than Shakespeare's other plays. It is not similar to *Hamlet* or *King Lear,* which are studies of individual men. *A Midsummer Night's Dream*, Chesterton points out, is a spirit among men. We can say it is the playfulness among people. This is a greater triumph than bitterness, anger, greed, etc.

In prison group therapy, "sparks" of smiles, laughter, and mirth gradually develop. Similar to any variable, this can get out of hand, not only with prisoners but with normal people, as Zimbardo (Sleek, 1996) learned.

The emergence of play appeared when one prisoner remarked, "Dr. Scott puts truth serum in his tea." Laughter was spontaneous from the members and from me. The backdrop for this comment is that I brought tea bags to each session. Several dynamics are indicated: (1) a family group, (2) we all like tea–it's a treat, (3) oral satisfaction, (4) they recognize the treat and say "thanks." Now, just prior to the prisoner's (John's) remark, another prisoner had said, "In this group I

Figure 7. This cartoon suggests what the "Heavy" (tough) group thought of their therapist.

don't hold anything back." A second prisoner echoed a similar remark. At that point, John made his remark about the tea. It was perfect timing. It was humorous. It was playful. And it remained a "mantra" forever. As the prisoners came to group, several would remark (with a smile), "Well, what's in your tea today? I better not start to talk."

In another group, the following cartoon was given to me. It is, I believe, well done and rather correct for the "Heavy Group."

At times, I would rise from my chair and stand behind a prisoner. Depending on the prisoner's psychological state—if paranoid, he'd say, "Doc, I can't take it now. Later." This was a clear diagnostic tool; in addition, it provided clinical material. Some others would say, "Hey, Doc, come and stand behind me." Fruitful discussions arose in an atmosphere of play; learning seemed to get "inside" more easily.

Duvall (1971), in the preface to the text *Alcohol and Health*, made, for me, a remarkably profound statement, "Man's desire to alter reality is one of the most ancient, persistent and understandable of human needs" (p. ix). If Duvall is correct, there is only one choice: good or poor avenues to an ASC (altered state of consciousness). For alcoholics, in spite of genetic and environmental variables, the driving force is to alter reality. This same holds, I believe, for prisoners. Treatment is one avenue that has the potential for altering (positively) the prisoner's reality—in Hatcher's (1990) thesis, presently (moral) and for the future (anagogical) aspects.

One prisoner summed up his change from group therapy in the following:

What I Like About Group Therapy

I know one thing right off the bat, is the comradery on the same subject, for around the room, is the only way I can receive the objectiveness of my peers. Whether I am pushing my peers too hard or too lightly, into answering their own questions with their own answers and not with others "answers." I'm not saying that the Change Agent hasn't got a lot of sage advise and wisdom, though, I am saying that if one of the subjects doesn't find the answer for him or hers own usage, that there won't be a sense of achievement for that student. I always get anxious and happy that it's my turn next in Dr. Scott's group, because I get to try out my answers on the entire group and on a psychologist. In the last year and a half, I've learned more about myself than in the last 15 years of captivity. Dr Scott's treatment has changed me from a convicts way of life to a treatment one.

Earlier in the chapter, we mentioned Anthony's (1968) treatment thesis that "people come to us depressed, deadened, defeated, and destroyed in order to be set free to play" (p. 299). Utilizing that format, we maintain that *prisoners come arrogant, aggressive, afflicted and adrift in order to play according to the rules of society.*

Chapter 10

PTSD vs PGE

PTSD, as readers easily recognize, is from DSM-IV (1994), meaning posttraumatic stress disorder. PGE will not be recognized. It is the author's idea, meaning "post growth experience."

In DSM-IV (1994), we read, "The essential feature of posttraumatic stress disorder is the development of characteristic symptoms following exposure to an extreme traumatic stressor involving direct personal experience of an event that involves actual or threatened death or serious injury, or other threat to one's physical integrity; or witnessing an event that involves death, injury or a threat to the physical integrity of another person; or learning about unexpected or violent death or injury experienced by a family member or other close associate" (p. 424). Several examples are provided for the purpose of assisting–correctly–for this diagnosis.

To fully grasp the history, changing opinions and complexities, Kinzie and Goetz (1996) have provided an exhaustive and informative article on PTSD, "A Century of Controversy Surrounding Posttraumatic Stress-Spectrum Syndromes: The Impact on DSM-III and DSM-IV." They wrote, "Many symptoms that have historically been related to trauma did not find a place in the DSM-IIIR (1987) or DSM-IV criteria: weakness, fatigue, and loss of will power..., headache..., and multiple psycho-physiological reactions, particularly gastrointestinal distrubance" (p. 173). Finally, they concluded, "There are few descriptions of dissociative symptoms, except amnesia, operating in post-traumatic states. This fact is recognized by the limited dissociative symptoms required for the diagnosis of PTSD in DSM-IV. In fact, DSM-IV reflects on the ongoing ambivalence of our profession in its decison to maintain dissociative disorders in a separate diagnostic group" (p. 174).

Peebles (1989) has argued, "Posttraumatic stress disorder, a term created by the American Psychiatric Association in 1980, is a modern buzz word" (p. 274). Following the above statement, Peebles presented notions why the term has been popular. One of the reasons given was that of "the demands of the legal system" (p. 275). Psychological/psychiatric reasons also existed. According to Peebles, "There was a search for a model of trauma that could account for a stress reaction in the absence of preexisting psychiatric pathology" (p. 277).

Among the various ideas contributing to this notion are the biological. In this area, Peebles noted "kindling." A brief review of kindling was given in Chapter 2 closely following Post's (1992) idea. Peebles selected other authors for her ideas. Later in this chapter we will return to the concept of "kindling."

The concept of PGE might simply be described as "an event in one's life that has lead to psychological growth (maturity)." The event is "lasting," that is, remains with the individual for years, having a positive effect in his/her life. DSM-IV (1994) comes closest to our PGE in Axis V which is described as used "for reporting the clinician's judgement of the individual's overall level of functioning" (p. 30). While on page 58, the GARF Scale (Global Assessment of Relational Functioning) is provided. A score of 81-100 indicates a "relational unit is functioning satisfactorily from self-report of participants and from perspectives of observers" (p. 758).

Our proposed PGE assumes a more active (proactive) approach. For instance, "an accounting" (awareness) of practicing an event (meditating, reading, exercise, etc.) which the individual judges as promoting his/her mental health. Barth (1986) reflected, "I have for years and years begun each day with Mozart and only then (aside from the daily newspaper) turned to my dogmatics" (p. 16).

There are also those lasting events—for good—which occur. Boorstin (1992) has recorded (a memory of Stravinsky's *The Rite of Spring*) that he, "remembered from his childhood on the Russian countryside as a time of sudden rebirth" (p. 502).

In an attempt to have the prisoners remember a positive event from the past, a memory of Mark Twain's was slowly read to them. Werge (1984), in his article, recorded that when Twain was a young boy, he asked his mother to quiet a slave boy "whose perpetual whistling and singing he found maddening" (p. 16). Twain's mother explained that the family was to be split up and "his singing helped forget his pain" (p. 16). Twain later recalled, "the incident stayed in my memory clean and sharp, vivid and shadowless all those slow drifting years" (p. 16). Following this, Twain reported that the young slave boy's singing "was not a trouble to me anymore" (p. 16).

The individual prisoner members of group therapy were asked, "Think back in your life and recall an event that had a positive effect on you for a period of time." They were given five to ten minutes.

PGE QUESTION RESPONSES

Group 1

Ted:	Can't think of anything. Well, my dad beat me. My uncle and aunt came and got me–kidnaped away. That was good.
Gary:	Nothing (Just had a session with his mother and inmate in which the mother reported her effort to care for Gary!)
Mike:	My stepmother would tell me, "You look good."
Mark:	My stepdad and I would take walks and he'd say, "No matter what, the thing that you have is your word. Keep it."
Ken:	My dad would say, "Do it yourself. Don't be dependent on others. You have to grow up. If you don't, you'll have problems all your life." I agree.
Willy:	"If you do a job, do it right," my dad said.
Red:	In high school, I was told I had sales ability.
Robbie:	I had a black belt. I was told, "Keep on working." That was good.
Ed:	My grandpa told me to respect women, but that's not true.

The prisoners were now asked: Remember a time you did something good for someone.

Ted:	I'm a good listener and that is helpful.

Gary: I told my niece that she should graduate from high school.

Mike: I wrote a letter to someone. Everyone seemed not to care for him.

Mark: I told my little cousin, "Don't get caught up in dope."

Ken: I'd helped around the house, inside with Mom and outside with Dad.

Willy: I was a coach and I'd encourage the kids.

Red: My roommate died last year and I went through it with him. He said, before he died, I was helpful.

Robbie: I took a class for Judo and I told the young students, "Listen to your parents."

Ed: I wrote a letter to a friend.

Group 2

("Recall something positive in your life.")

Sam: When my dad kicked me out of home, I was 14; my older sister took me in. She told me to forgive Dad. I don't think I have.

Abe: Nothing. Well, my son. He's the only one who writes to me.

Ben: A person I looked up to said, "There are things you won't want to do, but you'll have to do 'em."

Ken: My brother taught me how to survive when growing up.

Vince: In high school, my coach told me to be the best you can. That's good.

Herb: My stepbrother took me to ball games.

("When have you done something positive for someone?")

Sam: When my wife left, I tried to do the best I could for her. I did.

Abe: My son. I told him not to go to prison–like I have. Don't end up like me.

Ben: A neighborhood kid, 15, on drugs and rebelling, I said, "Have your own identity."

Ken: I cared for a and loved my son.

Vince: I helped my little sister one time.

Herb: I took my little bro places.

Group 3

("Recall something positive in your life.")

Andy: Nothing from my early years, but when I was arrested my parents gave me support. I couldn't tell 'em what I did.

Red: Nothing from early childhood. Of course, there might have been something I didn't recognize. Though I've been helped in prison.

Ted: When five years old, my mother told my brother and me not to play in the streets. "You might be killed." My brother played in the streets, and I began to cry. I thought he'd get killed.

John: When little, I enjoyed older people who'd tell stories about their life.

Jack: My mother told me not to get my girlfriend PG. I did. So I married her.

("When have you done something good for someone?")

Red: Nothing.
Ted: I like to help others.
Andy: Probably nothing.
John: I've helped others with money.
Jack: I've gone to high school to help a stepkid.

Group 4

("Recall something positive in your past life.")

Fred: I was lucky I grew up with a good family. It made me happy.

Chester: My parents loved me. That helped me not to be negative.

Andy: Dad instilled morals. My mom's ways have got me into trouble.

Dennis: Grandma told me to respect adults.
Ed: My uncle told me, "We love you."
Red: Nothing.

("When have you done something good for someone?")

Fred: I, when Dad was celebrating his birthday, I gave him a kiss.
Chester: I gave Christmas gifts to my mom.
Andy: I gave my brother some money.
Dennis: I saved the life of a kid who was drowning in a lake.
Ed: I helped a boy scout when I was patrol leader.
Red: Nothing.

Scanning the remembrances of these prisoners, the results appear most meager. Positive self-promoting events either from the self or from others seem, by and large, to have not been present in their lives.

Research, however, regarding negative, nonpromoting mental health, has shown constant evidence in this direction. Perhaps, Hankoff's (1987) research is typical in this arena. In comparison of male offenders versus normal controls, the former group "differed significantly from the normals, in being more dramatic, more often unpleasant in quality, and more often depicting disturbing or aggressive interaction or reciprocity" (p. 195). The issue is, how accurate is the offender group? Did they, in fact, undergo more negative events?

What hinges on this discussion is that of diagnosis. Recalling that one of the principle assumptions of PTSD is trauma. Peebles (1989) has stressed that "there was a search for a model of trauma that could account for a stress in the absence of a preexisting psychiatric pathology" (p. 277). Gabbard (1992) has argued that "the fact that one person will respond with PTSD to a situation that leaves no permanent mark on another reflects the fact that the subjective meaning given to the environmental stimulus is critical in effecting synaptic charges" (p. 992). However, biological aspects of the individual might be a variable in this puzzle.

A PTSD MEMORY BY A PRISONER

If we recall from Chapter 3 that one, if not the most, vigorous findings was that the prisoner responses regarding childhood were clearly negative. The question under consideration is: Does an early diagnosis (DSM-IV) of ADHD or learning disorders or communication disorders and/or conduct disorders lay the foundation for the recipability of PTSD? It would be a supposition that it does. By analogy the youngster's "psychological immune system" functions poorly. As a result, the future adult, in our case the future prisoner, has a readiness to impute negative meanings to events. In other instances, the negative early experiences are in themselves sufficient in producing PTSD. The following "story-incident" written by a prisoner underlies the severity of the event.

> One of the first things I can remember happened when I was about 3 yrs old. This was before the birth of the eldest 2 of my siblings, when my mother was married to my first stepfather. I really don't recall what started all of it off, but my stepfather came home late that night and I'm not sure where he'd been.
>
> I'm pretty sure he was drunk, because I seem to remember that he was staggering when he came through the front door and he yelled at me to go to my room. It seems as if nothing happened for a while, because I remember that I was playing when I heard my mother start yelling. But what really scared me was when I heard things hit the wall and shatter. Then I heard the sound of someone being slapped and my mother was screaming. That's when I ran into my closet and closed the door. For some reason I felt safe, like by sitting there in the dark against the corner I was safe.
>
> The yelling and screaming and slapping went on for a while before it finally stopped. I stayed in the closet for a little while before I came out. I'm not really sure how long. When I came out of my closet it was because I heard the front door slam.
>
> Laying there in the front room, beaten and bloody, was my mom. There were broken objects all over the room, and my mom was unconscious in the middle of the floor. I was in shock. All I could do was stand there and look. Stepfather wasn't anywhere around.
>
> Well, after trying to talk to my mom, and not knowing why she wouldn't get up I went out the front door and down the hall to my babysitters. I think she called the police, because all I remember after that is a blur of colored lights, and people surrounding me from all sides. After that my mom went to the hospital while I stayed with my babysitter for a couple days. When my mom came home, she was covered in bruises, both bodily and in spirit because she refused to talk about the incident even now. I still don't know what the argument was about. And even after it was all over, it was like nothing had happened. Because my stepfather came back and the incident was forgotten by everyone but my self.

The problem of remembering earlier life's experiences, framed in either good (positive) vs. bad (negative) has been reported by Scott (1971). He formulated a questionnaire for children (5-6 grades), high school students, alcoholics, mental patients, and normal individuals. Regarding alcoholics, both male and female, subjects judge that the sad event in their life was "deeper," more meaningful than the happy events they had selected. However, male alcoholics judged that they experience more happy events than sad events; not so for female alcoholics. Mental patients (defined as those in a psychiatric facility) judged that they experienced more sad events than happy events, according to both male and female respondents. This same population believed the sad event selected from their past life was deeper than the happy event they had chosen. For the normal population, both male and female subjects selected that they experience more happy events than sad events. Moreover, the happy event was "deeper" (more meaningful) than the sad event. Scott mentioned that he did not evaluate the objectivity of the respondents' lives. In other words, do nonnormal folks (alcoholics, mentally ill individuals—and prisoners) have more negative aspects in their past and present lives, or do they interpret (misinterpret) what is happening?

SOME RESEARCH ON MEMORY

This question prompts a further question: just how does one remember? Andreasen et al. (1995) have conducted research on the topic of remembering. In brief, these researchers reported their results on different types of memory. They termed autobiographical "episodic." "It is called episodic because it is composed of a series of events which are sequentially ordered in time" (p. 1577). Then compare episodic memory with "semantic memory which is impersonal and not time linked and comprises an individual's repository of general information" (p. 1577). They noted that "Episodic memory is probably uniquely human" (p. 1577).

At this juncture they introjected "free association." In this type of memory, although it is episodic, it is "personal, individual, and autonoetic." They describe this particular type of memory REST. REST means random episodic silent thinking. Further, "The acronym is intentionally ironic, indicating that the resting brain is both active and interesting" (p. 1577). These researchers have employed positron emission tomography which allows for changes in the brain's activity by means of measuring "indices of metabolic activity such as glucose utilization or cerebral blood flow" (p. 1577).

The efforts to subscribe different areas to the brain resulted in some complex findings. For example, two regions with nearly identical coordinates (episodic and REST memory) emerge in both these conditions: the medial inferior frontal (area 11) and the precureils" (p. 1583). They indicated that both types of memory "involve something personal and highly individual." What they next mentioned appears to be specifically pertinent for the prison population, namely, "This frontal region is known from lesion studies involved in social awareness and the ability to possess a value system and experience guilt" (p. 1584).

Allen and Lewis (1996) have suggested, based on the research of others, that "the left hemisphere plays a relatively greater role in mediating positive emotions and the right hemisphere plays a relatively greater role in mediating negative emotions" (p. 256). This is an attempted hypothesis regarding "the avenues" for positive and negative emotions. It does not indicate the relative amounts of negative and positive emotions.

We have gone into specifics regarding memory because it is not simply a general topic, but one with different types of memory, which utilize particular areas of the brain and suggested parts of the brain utilized for negative or positive emotions. As one views this relatively small amount of information, one quickly grasps the meager efforts at regarding this important arena for prisoners.

Kindling is an intriguing idea. In Chapter 2, some basic notions regarding kindling were given. Basically, Post (1992) was used. In his article, the notion of kindling was negative. The current quest is: any positive kindling? It occurs to us that great men and women have benefitted from positive kindling. Our first inclination is to point to individuals who have experienced a spiritual event which not only changed their lives, but was easily "rekindled."

Pontius (1993) has provided what certainly appears as a joyful kindling experience. In an attempt to establish his thesis, Pontius used the words of Proust taken from his autobiography. In that work, Proust mentioned the "unexplainable joy" he had recalling an event from early childhood. He had been sick. His mother brought him some sweets which he dipped into a cup of tea. Later, he visited an aunt. She offered him the same sweets (Petites Madeleines) dipped into tea. Proust reexperienced the original joy. Pontius concluded that Proust was ahead of his time. Presently the neurological phenomenon is employed to explain kindling.

Returning to our group of prisoners, the phenomenon of kindling would occur from time to time. All the phenomena were negative. They were reminded ("kindled") of a father figure, an officer, a peer, etc. They were, however, given the following weekly task: "Next week relate to the group the best thing that happened to you." This was an effort to make the group members aware of the positive things in their lives. It is our clinical impression that, at least, meager results occurred.

Years ago when our children were young, my wife and I "instituted a program." At every dinner, before the complaining, telling on one another, or the talking about the miseries of life at home or life at school, each child had to report on something good that day. It could be what happened to them ("Teacher called on me first") or what they did ("I caught the ball"), etc. etc. Of course, my wife and I had to "produce" something good. It was an excellent challenge for us. In our opinion, it produced fairly good results. Today, as grown adults, they still recall "that ordeal" laughing, and then say, "Today I...."

PRISONER RESPONSE TO MASLOW'S THESIS

Maslow (1970), as most readers know, became interested in the healthy personality. His phrase was "self-actualizing." From his research, he concluded "that practically all (though not quite all) have had loving lives, have loved and been loved" (p. 275). Furthermore, he added, "They need love less" than others. As we have noted from the previous chapters in this book and from the PET questionnaire, these prisoners seem to have received less love than the average child. Could we conclude that as a result as adults they would need more love?

Each group was read Maslow's above statement. The following are their replies.

Group 1

Ben: I agree with that statement. My parents had a mechanical attitude. I desired more, and as an adult I went to desperate things for love. I still feel those

	wants.
Jim:	Not loved when young. I had to find love as an adult.
Kevin:	I disagree with Maslow's idea. Well, I was loved by my grandparents when I was young, oh, say, for two years. But my mom didn't like me and that was for a long time. So, I guess I wasn't loved as a kid.
Charlie:	I wasn't loved as a kid and not used to it, so I don't need it.
Fred:	I was never loved. My dad died in a car wreck. Mom had to work. Six of us kids. And I've never been loved when older. I feel insecure.
Charlie:	I've a yearning for love–a passion in me–a wish that all people could be loved including me. This is different from what I first said.
Hank:	I didn't know my mom. Mom died. His second wife made him give us kids away before she'd marry him. I need love so much I'd do anything.
Kevin:	I wasn't loved and don't care.
Jim:	I've picked the wrong ones over and over.

Group 2

Charlie:	We need love, whether young or old.
Fred:	I need a lot of love.
Sam:	I had no love when young. I need more now, yet, I'm afraid. If they [women] hurt me, I'd hurt them.
Dave:	I wasn't loved when young. Now it's not necessary. Prison is hell.
Dr. Scott:	What you don't have you don't need?
Ed:	I disagree with you, Dave. I need a lot of love. I can't stand someone not loving me.
Ken:	No love as a kid and none now.
Ted:	I got hand-me-downs–a big poor family. As an adult, I need more love.
Dave:	You guys are wrong. If I have no car, I walk.
Ed:	You don't wish you had a car?
Dave:	If I can't fit with a bunch of rejects in prison, what can, how can I do on the outside?
Ed:	Love is great.

Charlie:	Yeah, it's like a jump start from another car.
Ted:	I had no love. I'm angry. A small thing can set me off, like my murder. I was called a name.
Ed:	You couldn't control it?
Charlie:	You felt degraded?
Ted:	I couldn't.
Ed:	Why couldn't you have talked it out?
Ted:	No, couldn't.
Dave:	Murder is murder. I deal with it–I murdered.
Sam:	Yeah, I know.
Ken:	I can understand the rage, but I had feelings for victims. I've been in prison a long time. There's no love in prison.
Charlie:	Yeah, Ken, same for me, but I need it.

Group 3

Sam:	I didn't have love when young. My mom said she loved me when I was in prison. I was shocked.
Jerry:	I had material love, but not emotional love. I need it more as an adult.
Fred:	Never loved when young. I don't need it now. I've never had it. If I got it, I'd be scared.
Martin:	When young, I had love. As an adult, I need less. I conditioned myself.
Dan:	I had love when young, but I'm only in my twenties now. My crime became an addiction.

Group 4

Joe:	I had love when I was young. Don't need it as much now. Well, yeah, maybe mental illness changes it. I'm mental.
Don:	I wasn't loved when young. I need more love now, like I need attention–never enough.
Ray:	I don't need love.
Dr. Scott:	You're a kind of friendly psychotic. You laugh and talk to yourself. You don't need anyone else?

Ray:	Yeah, it's my own world!
Mike:	I don't need people. I'm a loner now. I have hatred–a lot of hate.
Ben:	I was cared for. I agree with Maslow. He's right.
Charlie:	All my life not cared for. Mom didn't love. Sometimes I'm wicked.
Jack:	Not loved. I need love. I feel love from you, Dr. Scott.

REFLECTIONS

The diagnosis of PTSD can be difficult at times. A consideration of preexisting or nonpreexisting pathology is a variable frequently overlooked. Gabbard (1992) accurately has pointed out that one individual will undergo a PTSD diagnosis, while another individual will not, regarding the same situation. In keeping with the mission of psychiatry and clinical psychology, those individuals who have received a diagnosis of PTSD are studied. Scott (1989) has made an attempt in studying nonalcoholics from alcoholic homes. He concluded that six variables were associated with the results. One variable concerns the dominant parent. One respondent in the study reflected, "Mother was the most difficult. She was always upset, mad all the time" (p. 70). The father was alcoholic, but according to this respondent the psychiatrically sick mother was the dominant parent. A second variable was that of significant others outside the family. One male subject pointed out that his coach was the most important figure in his life. In this regard, Bowlby (1988) has agreed that, "The central task of developmental psychiatry is to study the endless interactions of internal and external" (p. 1). Surveys do not adequately answer Bowlby's challenging proposition.

PGE: A NEW CONCEPT

PGE appears to be a new concept for clinical psychology and psychiatry. An attempt was made to describe this concept adequately. Additionally, individual person's (Mark Twain, Barth, etc.) life style or significant impressions were employed to buttress the concept. Scott's

(1971) research about happiness was reported in which he found that alcoholics and mentally ill individuals do not, as a group, experience as much happiness as normal people. To those two above groups of unhappy people, we now add prisoners.

The complex question remains the facts of an individual's life. This is part of the formula, it seems that Bowlby suggested. What about the other half of Bowlby's (1988) formula–the internal? Is memory the key variable? A few pages back, an effort was made to track down the physiological aspects of memory. My work with patients, but especially with prisoners, has convinced me that their memory is selective. Selective implies if the memory is beneficial, the prisoner can be a victim and the memory will be employed to justify his emotions, thoughts, and actions.

Intermingled in memory, there is a physiological and a psychological reality, the important and intriguing concept of kindling. We hypothesized that kindling can be not only negative (as typically indicated), but positive kindling is a potential that requires a proactivity orientation to one's life. Suggestions were tendered in this regard.

Finally, Maslow's (1970) idea of the importance of love was accepted but questioned by some of the prisoners. On the whole, meager results were obtained. Obviously, the therapist cannot perform this function. He/she does have the opportunity to be positive when the prisoner patient makes progress in his emotions, thoughts, and behavior. This author routinely practiced this clinical technique.

Chapter 11

REFLECTIONS AND SUGGESTIONS

Clinical material voiced by the prisoner patients and the therapist raise significant and difficult questions. An attempt will be made to respond to those questions. At times, the reader might judge that the thesis or theme is carried on *ad infinitum*. I could reply, "*de gustibus non disputatur*," that is, in matters of taste, there's no dispute. Translated for the present purpose, it is our belief that themes, theses and treatment agendas are matters for dispute or argumentation. A forum for this phenomenon is critical. Most texts are either devoted to clinical data or to academic questions. Our present hope is to combine these two avenues. The propositions are somewhat independent. Hence, the reader can select those issues judged to be especially pertinent to him or her.

PROPOSITIONS

Treatment

In physical medicine, we are taught by physicians to accept various levels of treatment success. Recently, a major health agency shifted its focus from the infectious diseases to the more chronic ones (heart, cancer, and depression). It is our opinion, based on over twenty years of working with offenders in and out of prison, that the typical offender has for the most part a chronic disorder. Crime appears as both a social and personal disorder. Seemingly, both of these two phenomena are increasing. The appearance of crime made an early entry in the recorded pages of history. A valid conclusion: crime is chronic. In the last few years, crime appears to have a steady growth. Lacking a significant deterrent, crime will continue to rise. Why? What can be done?

Let us address the latter question on a more general level: does therapy work for the noncriminal individual? In our opinion, Seligman (1996) has provided a reasonable response. Briefly, Seligman evaluated the results of *Consumer Reports* (1995) in which 180,000 subscribers were sent a questionnaire regarding mental health; the rate of return was typical–13 percent: "About a third reported they had a mental health problem and about 40 percent of those saw a mental health professional" (p. 1073). Some of the results as indicated by Seligman were: (1) "The longer the therapy the more overall improvement" (p. 1074); (2) "The people who received long term therapy ... were more severely troubled, more emotionally disturbed and more likely to have psychodynamic treatment" (p. 1076).

Potential application for prisoners indicates in our judgement that prisoners are more disturbed than people in the general public. Secondly, if about 30-40 percent of the people in the general public were seeking a professional mental health person, I would estimate that 60-70 percent of prisoners are disturbed. These prisoners require and could benefit from seeing a professional mental health worker who has had special training. This is one of the main purposes for the present text. Kay (1996) has discussed a training plan for psychiatric residents for the current challenges. It was Kay's wish that among the positive characteristics, psychiatry would "attract the most curious of minds and the most caring of hearts" (p. 289). The reader easily recalls the title of this text, *Within the Hearts and Minds of Prisoners*. If Kay is seeking psychiatric residents with curious minds and caring hearts, these qualities are particularly required for working, in therapy, with prisoners.

Criticism raised against the results of the *Consumer's Report* (1995) was that it relied entirely on self-reports. In this regard, it lacked the other three legs of a good evaluation: blind diagnosis, complete assessment, and therapist evaluation. The current report has two of the four ingredients for a good evaluation, self reports of the prison patients and the therapist's evaluation. One must keep in mind the original condition of the prisoner when he entered group therapy. In physical medicine, to be able to walk for some patients is significant improvement, while for other patients it is entirely unimportant.

Personality Change?

At the close of his article, Seligman (1996) asked the question: long-term treatment has better results "for what kind of disorders? For what patients?" (p. 1087). In brief, can personality change?

McAdams (1994) has offered one of the better responses to this question. McAdams argued that personality can be reviewed at three levels:

A. Level 1: Traits

Traits are, typically, stable and remain so through a person's life. If change occurs, it is in the early years of life, say before 25-30 years of age. The following is one prisoner's thoughts regarding traits vs. nurture.

Pete's Idea on Traits vs. Nurture

First of all I'm not sure there really is such a thing as inherited personality traits. I tend to favor the nurture side in the argument between nature vs. nurture. But I really don't know that is not to say I blame myself being me on the way I was raised. I believe it was just a lot of complicated factors that lead me to make the choices I made. However there are some traits that I feel have been with me even before I thought of such a thing as traits or such. They are certain feelings or thoughts I've had since a little child.

Mainly there are 3 things. These are extreme shyness or self-consciousness. Anxieties or fearfulness of many different situations. And it seems at times lack of self-confidence or low self-esteem has always been around in varying degrees.

I think sometimes my drive for feminine affection is like a trait because it always seems to have been a major concern for me. And that's been one of my *personal concerns* since I can first remember. Why that is I'm not sure and don't care to hazard a guess at this time. But through my childhood, my teens and adulthood it's always seemed a main drive of importance for me to find that "Romantic Ideal Love." It is like I sought happiness outside myself. I believed for years that this was the way to be happy. In a way it was selfish, because I was centered on my own quest to find happiness. And as I went through the years the End came to justify the Means more and more and that is when my criminal thinking came in and perhaps existed before. The anxieties and insecurities certainly played their part and I made choices to go around these. To arrange my life around the society as I felt a secret outcast. As time went by I became more desperate and focus on my ideas as my only hope without looking at any possible alternatives to change. And without thinking about the girls, my victims. My concern was with myself and seeking my own happiness.

As far as my *life story* goes I look at that as a future I would hope for. Yes I think I did write or love the life I created for myself. I sought the nightmare I made for myself even though I looked through many delusions. My fatalistic self-defeating negativity was always at the back of my drive and it was self actualizing. Be that as it may, it does not mean I can not change albeit not without a lot of hard mental reconditioning that must be self activated by me. Because if I don't really want to change it won't happen.

I really have to have goals in life because without direction I'll falter. My goal is to be the best person I can be. Not the most self-satisfying but satisfied with myself.

So the difference between now and then is to be happy is found in my own self-respect. And to find self respect is to be part of human society and helpful. Not too cause others unhappiness. I can feel that way if I feel I am honestly working towards it but not at the expense of anyone else. That not what its about. Before I looked for respect or sought my esteem, confidence or what have you from my relationships.

B. *Level 2: Personal Concerns*

Essentially this level of personality is gleaned by "what the person wants, how that person goes about trying to get what he or she wants" (p. 304). In brief this level is termed motivational. The previous prisoner's thoughts indicate his struggle with traits versus what he wanted. The following patient's reflections more clearly spell out his methods of motivation. This prisoner relates how he used to go about getting what he wanted:

Henry's Method of Getting What He Wanted

Dr. Scott

Starting at age five, I can remember watching my younger brother playing in the streets on a wooden scooter, I was told to watch him, but I was also told not to play in the street at any cost. So, I stood there on the corner of the street crying my eye's out, because I didn't want to get into trouble and I didn't want to see my brother get hit by a car. My Mother finally heard my crying and came out and got my Little Brother out of the street. Age 6-7 were pretty complacent, in that nothing happened, that was big news to me. The only thing I can remember with any significance, is we were camping, and I got real sore leg cramps and my Mother thought it might be Polio, which was wide-spread in those days, but it was just sore muscles from running in the sand.

As you can see, I always looked for being victimized, whether by people, animals or my environment. I always needed people in my life or around me that would give me the security and protection that I felt I needed, even into childhood. And when that security was gone or not met, I would leave the area and I wouldn't return. I think I must have set up the victimizing of my situations and then I would get so involved in the victimization that I would forget how I had set it up in the first place. Before I got into treatment, I would always justify the murder.

Knowing now that I set myself up for feeling like I'm the victim of others, I will get rid of the feeling by reminding myself of how many victims I've brought forth myself.

C. Level 3: Life Narrative

McAdams (1994) summarized this level of personality by saying it "concerns the making of the Self" (p. 306). The life story (narrative) contains numerous themes and aspects. The reader is reminded that Chapter 1 mentioned the central focus given to prisoners' stories, narratives, and anecdotes. In fact, we noted the phenomenon of stories within stories. We were alerted by Zeanah and associates (1989) to their conviction of the Life Narrative. In this present book, prisoners were provided the opportunity to create a story–a fairy tale.

McAdams stressed "nuclear episodes or key scenes" (p. 307) of the Life Narrative. The key issues reveal much about the individual: loyalness, stability, willingness to change, etc. What I must underline is that "nuclear episodes" are for prisoners typically negative. As a consequence, the prisoner makes himself a victim of negative episodes. He utilizes this in his rationalizations for his ensuing behavior.

Finally, McAdams posed the most important question: "How does personality change at Level III? Here the data are virtually nonexistent" (p. 308). We attempted to respond to that question in Chapter 10 regarding PTSD vs PGE. The thesis proposed and seemingly correct was that negative events had a deeper impact on the prisoner's life than the positive events. As previously reported in Chapter 1 (Introduction) alcoholics and psychiatric patients also indicate more negative life experiences. Prisoners join these two groups.

Confirmation evidence to the above thesis has appeared from the work of Franz (1994). Franz's research was longitudinal. The psychological instrument used was the Thematic Apperception Test (TAT). Each card on the TAT has a picture. The task of the subject is to make up a story. Six different pictures were used in Franz's work. From ages 31 to 41, substantial changes occurred on the TAT. Franz wrote, "In this sample the evidence for change is strong, most of it depending with theorized age-related changes of middle-aged adults, some of it associated with normative life experience" (p. 244). In other words, age and experience of a normal or abnormal life (health, family, social turmoil, etc.) does influence changes of personality. We assume this same conclusion would be found with prisoners if they were given a series of TAT cards at the same ages of Franz's subjects.

Baumeister (1994) has researched changes in people. He has a key argument called "Crystallization of Discontent." He described this idea when he wrote, "Crystallization of discontent (is) a centrally important step in major life change" (p. 294). This means "the forming of associative links between problems, conflicts, costs, objection and other negative features" (p. 294). We have listened, we believe, to the forming of "crystallization of discontent" in group therapy. For example, one prisoner reflected, "There is nothing good about me. I've done it all...well, uh, there is something good in my life, my two daughters. But shit, I'm in prison." Months later in group therapy he said, with deep emotion (from his heart?), "I hate drug dealers. I used to be one. It kills people. I know. My daughters...when I get out, I'm out."

Another prisoner stated, "I made a mistake. I'm paying for it. I, well, yeah, I'd rather be in the ground." Still another prisoner said, with sincerity, "I was on drugs when I killed him. I used to use that as an excuse. Hell, I remember it clear as a bell. I'm glad I remember it. It's part of my history." We could change "my history" to narrative self. Later in group, he related, "I joined prison thinking when I first came. But, they, uh, well, all they want to do is play a game." Still later, after struggles with himself (a stand-up guy to himself), he became a type of Oedipus. (Oedipus had to know what happened; he didn't know.) He knew what happened—he had to "stand-up" (admit it) and change. We believe these are at least partial answers to McAdams's\ (1994) question regarding change.

Evil

We now enter into a difficult, complex, and debated area: Evil. Miller and C'de Baca (1994) learned that their interpretation of their findings depended on one's belief in God. They wrote, "It is here that we encounter the fascinating and sometimes discomforting boundary of psychology and spirituality" (p. 276). Our present touchy boundary is that between psychology and evil.

This topic is typically ignored by American psychiatry. Slovenko (1995) called attention to the fact that evil was not accepted for inclusion in DSM-IV (1994). The rationale given, "Evil wouldn't have a practical use and DSM-IV couldn't include all human activity" (p. 296).

Simon (1996) approached evil but failed to touch the topic. Perhaps the "psychiatric stove" was too hot to touch. Earlier in his book, Simon wrote, "Psychiatrists do not ordinarily apply the term evil" (p. 8). He left either religion or philosophy to deal with evil. Yet, Freud who was neither a philosopher nor a theologian felt free—as a lay theologian—to fully discuss and disagree with trained theologians. Although Jung is not included in Simon's index, he had a strong religious leaning. Ellenberger (1970) stressed that "one of Jung's favorite assertions: man is naturally religious. The religious function in man is powerful...as the instinct of sex and aggression" (p. 724). Two of the founders of dynamic psychiatry differ radically on the issues of religion and evil. Not much has changed in the present psychiatric scene.

Peck (1983) wrote *The People of the Lie: The Hope for Healing Human Evil*. According to Slovenko (1995), Peck was viewed, not as a psychiatrist, but as a religious author and ignored.

Coles (1990), a well-respected child psychiatrist, wrote that Perry Miller, "who, as my undergraduate tutor, inspired me to study religious and spiritual matters in spite of the powerful agnosticism I met with in post World War II medicine and psychoanalysis" (p. xix). Ablow (1992), in his book *To Wrestle with Demons*, offered a description of evil. He referred to a certain patient by asserting, "I am forced to confront the possibility of human evil, the idea that people might do horrible things to one another because they want to" (p. 140). Ablow summarized his own orientation to therapy when he stated, "I work at once in the house of medicine and the house of God" (p. 113).

In contrast to the typical American psychiatric stance, the *British*

Journal of Psychiatry requested an editorial on evil. The guest editor Prins (1994) suggested that "evil is being equated somewhat arbitrarily with serious criminal wrong-doing, gratuitous personal violence" (p. 298). In our opinion, Arieti (1972), the noted American psychiatrist (but born in Italy), had given one of the better summaries of evil. He has declared:

1. "Evil depends on man's choice" (p. 223).
2. "Evil has a much larger role in human life than is generally realized" (p. 223).
3. "The truth is that psychology and psychiatry have not studied evil as evil" (p. 224).
4. He then indicated that neither standard dictionaries of psychology or of psychiatry have the term evil. We can recall Slovenko's (1995) remark that evil is excluded from DSM-IV.
5. Arieti defined evil "as any undeserved suffering caused by man" (p. 222).

If we utilize the descriptive definitions of Arieti and Prins it appears that the following statements by prisoners indicate evil:

1. *Bill:* "I have a deep down hatred for people."
2. *Bob:* "It was time to kill someone. I didn't give a damn. Nothing to feel guilty about."
3. *Ben:* "Every real criminal has a cold heart."
4. *Bruce:* "Fuck the world. I hate everything."
5. *Buber:* "My victim died too quickly. I needed to enjoy his suffering longer."
6. *Brimson:* "Hatred makes me strong. I feel evil."
7. *Steve:* "I can see my cat's face, terrible. (He killed his cat.) I looked at the guy I was killing and I say too fucking bad."

Satre (1996) employed the phrase "moral monsters" in a lecture given at the American Society of Criminology. He argued that capital punishment is not justified for this designated group.

Hitler, Stalin, and other "leaders" of hate and evil have demonstrated the horror of manmade evil. Pipes (1996) obtained from the Secret Archives material written by Lenin. In Document 24, Lenin instructed that oppression "should be mercilessly suppressed" (p. 50). Specific instructions were: "Hang so the people can see" (p. 50). In Document 94, Lenin was alert to a drastic situation and used it as a tiger who waited for the pregnant moment, giving instructions that "of starving regions" was a good time to strike "with the most savage and merciless energy" (p. 153).

Brown (1994) has pointed out that the word "phtonus covers the spectrum of violent dislike for good, even to the point of homicide" (p. 802). Perhaps a working description of human evil might be (1) enjoying the suffering of others; (2) a hatred for the good things either in an abstract way or a focus on a specific person; (3) thinking of a time when hated action is most likely to frighten; and (4) not only a lack of guilt, but a ready justification for one's actions.

Brown (1982) has suggested the following thesis, "The psychological motivation for a killer is most often his dislike or fear of what his adversary is doing; but in dualism evil hates good because it is good, and evil does evil because like does like" (p. 443). Brown is a theologian. Seemingly this is not an exclusive theological thesis. Kagan (1996), a well-known and respected psychological researcher from Harvard has recently written, "I side with the majority of moral philosophers and some psychologists in suggesting that one of the unique qualities of homosapiens is the continual disposition to apply a symbolic good-bad evaluation to most events" (p. 905). Further on he argued that there is a difference between pleasure and moral motives. Kagan wrote, "The receptors and the neural circuits that mediate sweet tastes and soft textures are known to a large degree, but those that mediate pride or guilt remain mysterious" (p. 905).

Let's linger a bit longer on the turf of the mysterious. The dictionaries indicate that mystery is something unknown or that can't be explained. The world famous physicist Hawking (1992) has thoughtfully made the following distinction: "The way the universe began would be determined by the laws of science. I would have succeeded in my ambition to discover how the universe began. But I still don't know why it began" (p. 112). That is, as I interpret it, in Hawking's mind, as a physicist, he can't explain why the universe began; it's a mystery. Psychology and psychiatry have, aside from what Kagan noted above, a number of mysteries. For the present purpose, we select two: goodness and evil. Peck (1983) stated, "Goodness remains a mystery even greater than the mystery of evil" (p. 41).

In my effort to understand, I've utilized a Freudian metaphor–Freud's (1900) metaphor of the "dream's navel." Freud pointed out that even if a dream receives an excellent interpretation, some aspects are not understood. According to Freud, "there is a tangle of dream-thoughts which cannot be unraveled....This is the dream's navel, the spot where it reaches down into the unknown" (p. 525). Hence, whether it is Hawking or Freud or Peck, plus a host of others, we do not understand some things. Evil is one of the unknowns, whether it is natural or supernatural. As the doctor says in Shakespeare's (1967) *Macbeth,* "This disease is beyond my practise" (Act V, Scene I).

Some readers might object to the Freudian idea of the "dream's navel," while other readers might be quick to point out *Hamlet* was written only with a knowledge of medieval medicine (Shakespeare, 1963). OK! Let these readers utilize the thesis of the black hole of modern physics–from which nothing can escape.

Creativity

As indicated previously, a most pleasant surprise was the creativity of these prisoners concerning fairy tales. Winnicott (1965) has insisted, "Only the True Self can be creative" (p. 148). Utilizing this assumption these prisoners did experience, to a degree, their True Self. Scott (1997) has argued that one significant phenomenon of group therapy with prisoners is that of providing an environment for the True Self to emerge and grow.

Sternberg and Lubart (1996) have an excellent article concerning creativity. Among their many findings was "one needs an environment that is supportive and rewarding of creative ideas. One could have all of the internal resources needed to think creatively, but without some environmental support (e.g., a forum for proposing those ideas), the creativity that a person has within him or her may never be displayed" (p. 684). It is my opinion that the prison system–as such–does not foster creative ideas by prisoners. Some of the classes held within the prison do provide an opportunity for learning. The main thrust of the prison is to keep the rules.

The present group of prisoners were prepared by having read to them selected portions of two fairy tales, *The Velveteen Rabbit* (Williams, 1981) and *The Fisherman and the Genie* (Bettelheim, 1976). A discussion followed each of the fairy tales. I then suggested that they create a fairy tale of their own. All did except one prisoner–he couldn't write.

Sternberg and Lubart (1996) found that creativity not only is personal, but it varies from one profession to another. They indicated that philosophy professors have the "ability to toy imaginatively with notions" while physics professors have "the ability to find order in chaos" (p. 683). What can be said for some "professors of crime?" For several years I have listened to criminals discuss their creative ideas regarding how "to peel a bank" (break into a bank). They have the ability to "rip off a store" and are probably most pleased in "cheating cheaters," etc. For the present group of prisoners, the suggestion to create a fairy tale was a pleasant and somewhat easy task.

Sternberg and Lubart have given an excellent summary of creativity. Yet, for me, the notion of Maslow (1963) that the truly creative "in the inspirational phase...lives only in the moment" (p. 5). In the chapter on prisoners' creation of fairy tales, I suggested some of the fairy tales that have that characteristic.

Love

I mentioned above how pleasantly surprised I was with the prisoners' creative ability. My biggest disappointment was associated with these prisoners and love. The results of the PET on the question of love revealed narcissism and/or lack of love.

Later, I read the last four lines from Robert Frost's poem, "The Lesson for Today." Frost (1971) described his own epitaph. The last line was, "I had a lover's quarrel with the world" (p. 280). Untermeyer commented that Frost would question and critique the world, "but always with understanding, always with earnest love" (p. 24). The last line underlined that one can argue and disagree with the world but never with hate.

PRISONERS AND THEIR RELATION TO THE WORLD

The above was read three or four times. Then two groups of prisoners were asked to indicate their feelings toward the world.

Group 1

Sam: In prison I have hatred for the staff and other inmates. Regarding the world, I'm confused.
Steve: Before my crime, okay. Then I blamed the world and everything else.
Bill: Fuck the world, is the way I feel. Hate!
Ben: Angry and a lot of hatred.
Bob: The world has treated me okay.
Bryon: My quarrel was with women.
Dave: I'm...damn angry.
Zeke: I was angry and kinda crazy.
Fred: The world sucks. I hate it.

Group 2

Paul: I'm confused about the world. This group is making me face myself and I'm scared.
Lew: I don't like the world—or anything.
Mike: Prison is a lot better than the world, but I thought I'd get raped.
Red: I came here so young, I don't really know the world. Prison is my world. If I ever get out, but, but, if I don't get out, I'd like to get someone in here to kill me.
Harry: Nothing good in prison and a hell of a lot of hatred out in the world.

As can be seen, the majority of these two prisoner groups have little love for the world. Generally, there is hatred and anger. Not only the above prisoners, but the majority of offenders have a gradation of anger and hate for the world. On the other hand, the majority have been sexually active but lack affection of a mature type for their sexual object. Today there are lecture-type programs for offenders. Perhaps one of the most popular is "Anger Management."

Many years ago when working with delinquent girls housed in a facility, one girl during a group therapy session reflected, "no one ever gave me a love lesson." She had been sexually active, but according to her never had love. This statement appears to be typical for many and perhaps the majority of prisoners.

At times we reviewed the early life of these groups of prisoners. It is always a question concerning accuracy of early life. The major theme can be summed by one prisoner, "I've never been in love. I yearn for a deep love. I think those of us never loved can love and be loved. Most of us believe we didn't get enough love when young." Others expressed themselves by saying, "I didn't know my mom and dad. My parents were divorced. I was put in a foster home. I need love so much." Another prisoner reflected, "Not love. I need love now. Dr. Scott, I feel love from you." One prisoner expressed himself by saying in a depressed mood, "All my life I was not cared for. Sometimes I wished I hadn't been born...."

A PROPOSED COURSE FOR PRISONERS

Utilizing the assumption that many of these prisoners either never had "a love lesson," or if they had didn't benefit, what is to be done? First, change of "courses" demanded that prisoners and offenders take must be made. An example is "Anger Management." Of greater benefit, I believe, would be a course entitled "Love Lessons." Tentatively, the following course outline comes to mind:

1. In Maslow's (1970) chapter, "Love in Self-Actualizing People," his first sentence reads, "It is amazing how little the empirical sciences have to offer on the subject of love" (p. 181). Sexuality is discussed. He stated that "the Freudian tendency to derive love from sex or identity from it is a bad mistake" (p. 190).

    A second reference, R. May's (1969) *Love and Will*, is critically important. Chapter V ("Love and the Daimonic") opens vistas of new ideas. For example, "The Greek concept of daimon... included the creativity of the poet and artist as well as that of the ethical and religious leader, and is the contagious power which the lover has" (p. 123).

2. The second portion of "Love Lessons" would include two or three couples regarding their married life–love, sex, money, in-laws, children, work, anger, etc. The couples would not only offer a "romantic-rosy" future but would reflect on their happy life as lived.

3. Erikson's (1964) Eight Stages of Life would be explained and explored. Each prisoner would need to know his "stage" and what is hindering him from advancing to the next stage.

Perhaps some readers might be inclined to think that I'm riding a hobby-horse "built" from my imagination. Not quite. Farley (1996), recent past president of the APA (American Psychological Association), stated, "In APA I believe it is probably time for a division on love and sexual behavior to help give some focus to this big topic" (p. 774). It is strongly suggested that any serious professional worker with prisoners or offenders would become a member of this new APA division.

APPENDIX I

PET (PRISON EXPRESSION TEST)

Example 1

1. **Prison life is** difficult at the time because I don't know if my life is in jeopardy because of the jacket I've been given.

2. **My childhood** for the most part was a happy one, except for the constant competetivness of trying to prove to peers that I was as good as the other most popular kids in the school.

3. **The worst thing that ever happened to me** is that I have been falsely accused and convicted and imprisoned for a crime that I did not comitt. And no one wants to help me, because they think I'm in denial.

4. **The best thing that ever happened to me** is that I was raised by two parents that love me very much and my family supports me.

5. **My mind** is currently in turmoil because of my recent breakdown, it's functioning better each day, but still needs work.

6. **Grandfather** has been dead before I was born, but my stepgrandfather (Lou) was real good to me and gave me "rocks" for my collection.

7. **I love** the Lord my God and, thank him that I was made in his image, and I love people and care for my fellow man.

8. **I feel a victim** is a person that has been mistreated, abused, or not given proper justice. A victim should not live in it, but rise above his injustice and become a survivor.

9. **My sexual life** is normal, but as I've gotten older, agape love is more important.

10. **Behind my back people say** things about me, not knowing that I'm telling the truth about my case. I've learned not to listen and ignore them.

11. **I spend most of my time** reading spiritual books and the Bible. I also spend

a lot of time brooding over how I've been abused by our justice system and others that lied to send me to prison.

12. If I could change one thing about me it is to stop dwelling on things that I can't control and work on what I can to improve my character.

13. I daydream about having Bar-B-Ques with my family and fishing with my kids on a sunny day up at North Fork.

14. Santa Claus reminds me of the Holiday Season and the spirit of giving; especially giving present to my kids at Christmas and spreading good cheer to all mankind.

15. God is the creator of all that is. He is Love and loves us enough to send His Son to die in the flesh so that my sins are forgiven.

16. Death is a part of living. Knowing I'm right with the Lord takes the sting out of death. I'd still like to live to be an old man.

17. I'd rather change other people than myself but since I can't, I'll work on my own life and maybe I can encourage other's to do the same.

18. When I was a teenager I was a Champion wrestler and admired by my peers, when I got injured, the walls came tumbling down.

19. I'm most proud about my integrety to continue to be honest and live right and continue to be good example to my children.

20. I'm most guilty about going to the prison administration.

21. My dreams at night are not usually pleasant. I usually feel in danger in my dreams.

22. Criminals are not all the same. Society needs to treat them individually and not stereotype them. Each case is different.

23. My greatest talent is the fact that I'm versatile, and am mediocre in many things and I have a lot of good to offer to society.

24. Laws in this country are made to uphold the mores of society. The more paganistic America becomes, the more laws will need to govern people.

25. My mother died when I was 20 months old, but God blessed me with a wonderful stepmother that is the greatest Mom in the whole world. and I love her very much.

26. Music plays an important part in my life. It is medicine to the mind and soul.

27. What I most love to see all my family together enjoying each other's company at a get together, dinner party, or camping trip.

28. My father is very concerned for me. He 79 yrs old, in a nursing home and he prays I'll get out of prison & spend some time with him before he departs from this world.

29. **What I don't understand about me is** why I have to continually have other people praise me for a good job, or I don't feel good about myself.

30. **My spouse** is now my ex-wife and her lies put me in prison. I don't hate her, but I dislike what she did to me.

31. **My sense of humor** is usually centered around all the funny or stupid little things we do as humans.

32. **Five years from now** I'd like to be out of prison, own my own small business, and be well on my way to helping other family members.

33. **I feel best when** I realize that my Lord is watching over me, and hopefully, soon I'll be back home with my family.

34. **My favorite novel is** usually short stories from condensed books in Readers Digest. Non in particular.

35. **Grandmother** I have or had 3 grandmothers. They were all special to me. They all loved me and spent time w/me. Great!

36. **The person I most love is** my sons. I also love my mother & father.

37. **One value I'll never give up** is putting the Lord first in my life, knowing that all good things come from Him.

38. **I can't stop thinking of** how people lied to put me in prison and how people may want to harm me or kill me because of the supposide crime.

39. **When I was a child, my mother's chief value was** to be honest and take care of my responsibilities.

40. **When I was a child, my father's chief value was** to teach us boys how to make a living and to enjoy life.

41. **Parenthood** is a privilage that I enjoy, not a pain. I'm proud to be a good loving, caring, & responsibile father.

42. **What I don't want to tell you** is that I don't trust any of you as far as I can throw you, until you show me otherwise.

43. **What I most want to tell you** is you need to believe me and help me overcome my fears and phobias.

44. **You can help me to** overcome my fears & paranoias about people wanting to kill me and investigate my case to see that I've been telling you the truth all along.

45. **I know I can help myself more if I would** trust and have more faith in God's promises and gain courage to take risk in life.

46. **Spiritual life** is very important to me. I believe that my soul needs nourishment from Gods Word and His guidance.

47. **The person who most loves me** My boys.

48. Pets <u>I like them, but I don't like to have to take care of them, so I'll just pet the dogs & my Mom's house.</u>

49. My problem is <u>I'm my own worse enemy and I'm hard on myself. I have paranoia & fears about being killed.</u>

50. I think it is caused <u>because I don't think I have as much to offer as other people do. Looks, strength, talents, intellegance. I have a problem w/my thought patterns.</u>

51. If I didn't have the problem <u>I would be much happier. And I wouldn't have to compete with everyone I come in contact with. That wears me out. I take life to serious, and I'd like to laugh more, but I'm not real good at telling jokes. I haven't found my notch in life and that upsets me. Why can't people like me, just because I'm a nice guy and I really care about other's and would do just about anything for anyone to feel accepted and valued by other's.</u>

52. The time I turned down good advise was <u>not to leave this group.</u>

53. I'll never change unless <u>I stop being paranoid.</u>

PET Test
Composed and compiled by Dr. Edward M. Scott

PET (PRISON EXPRESSION TEST)

Example 2

1. **Prison life is** boring and is safe and easy cause you don't have nobody breaking in plus no responsibilities

2. **My childhood** was very bad a lot of physical and mental abuse

3. **The worst thing that ever happened to me** was me being sexually abused.

4. **The best thing that ever happened to me** that I became an uncle.

5. **My mind** is constantly racing with thoughts of my past and other thoughts.

6. **Grandfather** is a retired logger.

7. **I love** my family but not as much as I should.

8. **I feel a victim** of abuse

9. **My sexual life** was very loose on the streets

10. **Behind my back people say** that I am no good

11. **I spend most of my time** in my cell reading and writing stuff from out of my mind.

12. **If I could change one thing about me it is** the manipulative tactics I use to get my way.

13. **I daydream about** the times I was hitchiking across the United States and being free with family

14. **Santa Claus** is not real

15. **God** is a personal relationship with me

16. **Death** does not scare because it's part of life.

17. **I'd rather change other people than myself** because it's easier to focus on others' problems than mine.

18. **When I was a teenager** I was involved in crime and ended up going to a juvenile detention center

19. I'm most proud about the few accomplishments I have made

20. I'm most guilty about scaring other people such as my crime victims

21. My dreams at night are sometimes sexual or self destructive or a combination of both.

22. Criminals get away with a lot especially myself.

23. My greatest talent is that I am good with kids

24. Laws in this country are unjust especially when murders get off scottfree.

25. My mother is a very loving, caring, and supportive person in my life.

26. Music to me is a way to escape into my own little world.

27. What I most love to see a sunset down by the beach

28. My father was a very mean person when he drank and was not supportive.

29. What I don't understand about me is why I can do good for so long than I mess up to come back to prison

30. My spouse I don't have one

31. My sense of humor is really important and other people like it to

32. Five years from now I would like to be back on the streets with my family.

33. I feel best when I'm under the influence of alcohol

34. My favorite novel is I don't have one

35. Grandmother died along time ago.

36. The person I most love is nobody

37. One value I'll never give up is my relationship with Jehovah

38. I can't stop thinking of my crime and how to put fear into my victims.

39. When I was a child, my mother's chief value was working

40. When I was a child, my father's chief value was his alcohol

41. Parenthood is something that two people really need to know how to do.

42. What I don't want to tell you nothing

43. What I most want to tell you is about my family

44. You can help me to learn to face myself and the problems that I have

45. I know I can help myself more if I would learn to face reality and not run from my problems.

46. Spiritual life is something to be taken seriously

47. **The person who most loves me** is God

48. **Pets** are fun but certain ones can be a pest

49. **My problem is** I manipulate to get my way.

50. **I think it is caused** from part of the disorder I have.

51. **If I didn't have the problem** I'd be much happier with myself

52. **The time I turned down good advise was** when I went beserk and committed my crime

53. **I'll never change unless** I decide that I want to change and I get tired of coming to prison.

PET Test
Composed and compiled by Dr. Edward M. Scott

APPENDIX II

FANTASY

by Joey

Fantasy is a very large part of a sex offender's dynamics, which are made up of thoughts and feelings. A fantasy to me is something I am aroused to that I think about in order to fulfill my needs sexually. A fantasy to me can be either a person that I am aroused to that I would like to do something sexual with, or a memory or flashback of something I have done in the past.

I am an exhibitionist, who has been convicted of public indecency. I exposed myself (penis) to a woman who was walking down the street minding her own business. This is not the only victim I have created. I have many victims of obscene phone calls, voyeurism (looking at women from outside their houses), exhibitionism, sexual assault, and even attempted rape, all of which were never reported or I was never charged with. Of all the 350+ victims I have created they all started with a thought or urge inside my head that I did not or could not control. The fantasies that I created inside my head came to a point where they were not enough for me, I had to do them! It is almost like a balloon that explodes after it is blew up so many times.

My fantasies consisted of me showing my penis to women and them wanting to have sex with it, at first. Once I continued to do this behavior it was not enough, so I fantasized about other things, because I was getting no results from my actions of exposing.

At this point I was not aware of the fact that I was progressing into a very hideous monster who preys on innocent women. I knew I was doing something wrong, but I quickly put those thoughts aside because "women like this and I am having fun doing it."

Appendix II

I had a live-in girlfriend at this time and yet I fantasized about having someone else, more attractive, so I used my girlfriend for sex only. In the meantime I was out touching women hoping for a "positive response" and when I did not get it, I tried and tried again.

During the time that I had progressed to the point that I was touching and grabbing women in public places, I had been convicted of the exposing charge and placed on probation, and was attending groups for sex offenders. I did not care. I continued to touch and fondle women in public and even began to stalk women by masturbating in my car downtown, fantasizing about sex with whoever it was that I was watching. I had started fantasizing about an actual rape at the time I entered a woman's house that I had voyeured on before. I went through her personals and masturbated in her house. I still occasionally fantasize about hiding under her bed till she goes to sleep and raping her.

The important thing to understand for me is that then I did not understand "fantasy" or the wrong criminal thinking that I had, until I started actual treatment and wanting to change. I am sure I don't yet understand everything about myself or sex offenders in general yet, but I do understand that a sex offender's fantasy structure is a whole hell of a lot different than that of the normal citizen, and if not recorded or monitored, or even brought out into the open, fantasy does indeed turn into reality for a sex offender, like myself. I admit to being a potential rapist or murderer, because I recognize that I have progressed to the point where this is what I fantasize about, this is what I am now aroused to and will do if I don't let it out and share my frustration and stressors with other people. I believe a lot of fantasies are triggered by feelings or emotions that are involved with something going on in that individual's life. For me a lot of my fantasies are "triggered" by anger. When I am angry at someone I need to get back at them, so maybe I can't physically, so I pick on someone weaker in my head. It usually turns out to be a woman. I don't want to do this anymore.

REFERENCES

Ablow, K.: *To Wrestle With Demons.* Washington, D.C., American Psychiatric Press, 1992.

Allen, J. & Lewis, L.: A conceptual framework for treating traumatic memories and its application to EMDR. *Bull of Menninger Cl, 60*:238-263, 1996.

American Psychiatric Association: *Diagnostic and Statistical Manual,* 3rd ed revised. Washington, DC, American Psychiatric Association, 1987.

American Psychiatric Association: *Diagnostic and Statistical Manual,* 4th ed. Washington, DC, American Psychiatric Association, 1994.

Andreasen, N.: *The Broken Brain.* New York, Harper and Row, 1984.

Andreasen, N.: O'Leary, D; Cizadlo, T.; Arndt, S.; Rezai, K.; Watkins, G.; Boles Ponto, L., and Hichwa, R.: Remembering the past: Two facets of episodic memory explored with Position Emission Tomography. *Am J Psychiatry, 152*:1576-1585, 1995.

Anthony, J.: Reflections on twenty-five years of group psychotherapy. *Int J Group Psychotherapy, 18*:277-301, 1968.

Arieti, S.: *The Intrapsychic Self.* New York, Basic Books, 1967.

Arieti, S.: *The Will to be Human.* New York, Quadrangle Press, 1972.

Azar, B.: Research plumbs why the "talking cure" works. *Monitor,* Washington, D.C., American Psychological Association, 1994.

Barth, K.: *Wolfgang Amadeus Mozart.* Grand Rapids, Wm. B. Eerdmans, 1986.

Baum, L. Frank.: *The Wizard of Oz.* New York, World, 1972.

Baumeister, B.: The crystallization of discontent in the process of major life change. In Heatherton, T. and Weinberger, J. (Eds.): *Can Personality Change?* American Psychological Association, 1994, pp. 281-298.

Bettelheim, B.: *The Informed Heart.* Glencoe, Free Press, 1960.

Bettelheim, B.: *The Uses of Enchantment.* New York, Alfred A. Knopf, 1976.

Bible: *Jerusalem Bible.* New York, Doubleday, 1966.

Boethius, A.: *The Consolation of Philosophy.* New York, Penguin Books, 1986.

Boorstin, D.: *The Creators.* New York, Vintage Press, 1992.

Bowlby, J.: Developmental psychiatry comes of age. *Am J Psychiatry, 145*:1-10, 1988.

Brown, R.: *Crises Facing the Church.* New York, Penguin Books, 1975.

Brown, R.: *The Epistles of John.* New York, Doubleday, 1982.

Brown, R.: *The Death of the Messiah.* New York, Doubleday, 1994.

Carpenter, W. and Strauss, J.: The mind, the body and the immune system. *The Harvard Mental Health Letter, 8*:No 7, 1-3, 1992.

Cervantes, M.: *Don Quixote,* 7th printing. New York, The Viking Press, 1958.

Chesterton, G.: *The Common Man*. New York, Sheed and Ward, 1950.
Coles, R.: *The Call of Stories*. Boston, Houghton Mifflin, 1989.
Coles, R.: *The Spiritual Life of Children*. Boston, Houghton Mifflin, 1990.
Consumer Reports: Mental health: Does therapy help? *Consumer Reports, Nov*:734-739, 1995.
Dies, R.: Models of group psychotherapy: Shifting through confusion. *Int J Group Psychotherapy:42*,1-17, 1992.
Dunne, J.: *Time and Myth*. Notre Dame, University of Notre Dame Press, 1973.
Dunne, J.: *The Reasons of the Heart*. New York, Macmillan, 1978.
Duvall, M.: Preface. In S. Rosenberg (Ed.): *Alcohol and Health*. Rockville, 1971.
Eisenberg, L.: The social construction of the human brain. *Am J Psychiatry, 152*:1563-1575, 1995.
Ellenberger, H.: *The Discovery of the Unconscious*. New York, Basic Books, 1970.
Erikson, E.: *Childhood and Society,* 2nd ed. New York, W.W. Norton, 1964.
Farley, F.: From the heart. *American Psychologist, 51*:No 8, 772-776, 1996.
Favazz, A. & Simeon, D.: Self-mutilation. In Hollander, E. & Stein, D. (Eds.): *Impulsivity and Aggression*. New York, John W. Ley & Sons, 1994.
Fine, R.: A critical examination of the concept of acting-out in the neurosis of our time. In Milan, D. & Goldman, G. (Eds.): *Acting-Out*. Springfield, Charles C. Thomas, 1973.
Frank, F.: *Persuasion and Healing*. Baltimore, John Hopkins University Press, 1973.
Franz, C.: Does thought context change as individuals age? In Heatherton, T. & Weinberger, J. (Eds.): *Can Personality Change?* Washington, D.C., American Psychological Association, 1994.
Freud, A.: Mechanisms of defense, in the analysis of defense. In Sandler, J. & Freud A. (Eds.): *The Ego and the Mechanisms of Defense*, New York, International Universities Press, 1985.
Freud, S.: The interpretation of dreams. Strachey, J. (Trans.).: *The Complete Psychological Works*. London, Hogarth Press, 1900.
Freud, S.: *Group Psychology and the Analysis of the Ego*. New York, W. W. Norton, 1959.
Freud, S.: Humor. Strachey, J. (Trans.).: *The Complete Psychological Works: The Standard Edition, 21*:161-166, 1974.
Frost, R.: *Robert Frost's Poems*. New York, Washington Square Press, 1971.
Gabbard, G.: Psychodynamic psychiatry comes of age. *Am J Psychiatry, 149*:991-998, 1992.
Guze, S.: Biological psychiatry: is there any other kind? *Psychol Med, 19*:315-323, 1989.
Halleck, S.: American psychiatry and the criminal. *Int J Psychiatry, 6*:185-208, 1968.
Halleck, S.: *The Politics of Therapy*. New York, Science House, 1971.
Hankoff, L.: The earliest memories of criminals. *Int J Offender Therapy and Comparative Criminology, 31*:195-201, 1987.
Hatcher, E.: Dante, psychoanalysis and the (erotic) meaning of meaning. *Bull of Menninger Cl, 54*:353-367, 1990.
Hawking, S.: *A Brief History of Time*. New York, Bantam Books, 1992.
Heuscher, J.: *The Psychiatric Study of Fairy Tales*. Springfield, Charles C. Thomas, 1963.

Holton, C.: Once upon a time served: therapeutic application of fairy tales within a correctional environment. *Int J Offender Therapy and Comparative Criminology, 39*:210-221, 1995.

Huck, C.: *Children's Literature.* New York, Holt, Rinehart & Winston, 1979.

Kagan, J.: Three pleasing ideas. *American Psychologist, 51*: 901-908, 1996.

Kay, J.: New challenges to the faculty in the education of psychiatrists. *Bull of Menninger Cl, 60*:285-295, 1996.

Kemker, S. & Khadivi, A.: Psychiatric education: Learning by assumption. In Ross, C. And Pam, A. (Eds.): *Pseudoscience in Biological Psychiatry.* New York, John Wiley & Sons, 1995.

Kinzie, D. & Goetz, R.: A century of controversy surrounding posttraumatic stress-spectrum syndromes: The impact on DSM-III and DSM-IV. *Journal of Traumatic Stress, 9*:159-179, 1996.

Ludwig, A.: Altered states of consciousness. *Arch Gen Psychiatry, 15*:225-234, 1966.

Lynch, W.: *Images of Hope.* New York, Mentor-Omega Book, 1965.

MacIntyre, A.: *After Virtue.* Notre Dame, University of Notre Dame Press, 1984.

Maslow, A.: *The Creative Attitude.* Psychosynthesis Research Foundation. "Valmy," PO Box 3895, Greenville, DE,1963.

Maslow, A.: *Motivation and Personality.* New York, Harper & Row, 1970.

Mason, H.: *Gilgamesh.* New York, New American Library, 1970.

May, R.: *Love and Will.* New York, W.W. Norton, 1969.

McAdams, D.: Levels of stability and growth in personality across the life span. In Heatherton, T. & Weinberger, J. (Eds.): *Can Personality Change?* Washington, D.C., American Psychological Association, 1994, pp. 315-330.

Meissner, W.: *Ignatius of Loyola.* New Haven, Yale University Press, 1992.

Meuller, G.: The criminological significance of Grimm's Fairy Tales. In Bottingheimer, R. (Ed.): *Fairy Tales and Society: Illusion, Allusion and Paradigm.* Philadelphia, University of Pennsylvania Press, 1986, pp. 217-227.

Miller, W. and C'de Baca, J.: Quantam change: Toward a psychology of transformation. In Heatherton, T. & Weinberger, J. (Eds.): *Can Personality Change?* Washington, D.C., American Psychological Association, 1994, pp. 253-280.

Palermo, G.: *The Faces of Violence.* Springfield, Charles C. Thomas, 1994.

Palermo, G. & Scott, E.: *The Paranoid: In and Out of Prison.* Springfield, Charles C. Thomas, 1997.

Peck, M.: *People of the Lie: The Hope for Healing Human Evil.* New York, Simon & Schuster, 1983.

Peebles, M.: Posttraumatic stress disorder. *Bull of Menninger Cl, 53*:274-286, 1989.

Pipes, R.: *The Unknown Lenon.* New Haven, Yale University Press, 1996.

Plato: *The Meno Translated by W. Guthrie.* New York, Penguin Books, 1956.

Plato: Symposium. In Edman, I. (Ed.): *The Philosophy of Plato.* New York, Random House, 1956.

Pontius, A.: Overwhelming remembrance of things past: Proust portrays limbic kindling by external stimulus–literary genius can presage neurological patterns of puzzling behavior. *Psychological Reports, 73*:615-621, 1993.

Post, R.: Transduction of psychosocial stress into the neurobiology of recurrent affective disorder. *Am J Psychiatry, 149*:999-1010, 1992.

Prins, H.: Psychiatry and the concept of evil. *Brit J Psychiatry, 165*:297-302, 1994.

Pruyser, P.: *The Play of the Imagination.* New York, International Universities Press, 1983.

Rennie, D.: Storytelling in psychotherapy: the clients' subjective experience. *J Psychotherapy, 31*:234-243, 1994.

Samenow, S.: *Inside the Criminal Mind.* New York, Times Books, 1984.

Sandler, J. & Freud, A.: *The Analysis of Defense.* New York, International Universities Press, 1985.

Satre, T.: Capital punishment, justice and moral monsters. Lecture given at the American Society of Criminology Annual Meeting, November 21 at Chicago, 1996.

Scott, E.: *Struggles in an Alcoholic Family.* Springfield, Charles C. Thomas, 1970.

Scott, E.: *An Arena for Happiness.* Springfield, Charles C. Thomas, 1971.

Scott, E.: Group therapy with convicts on work-release. In Scott, E. & Scott, K. (Eds.): *Criminal Rehabilitation . . . Within and Without the Walls.* Springfield, Charles C. Thomas, 1973, pp. 147-167.

Scott, E.: Group therapy in a state prison. In Scott, E. & Scott, K. (Eds.): *Criminal Rehabilitation . . . Within and Without the Walls.* Springfield, Charles C. Thomas, 1973, pp. 93-111.

Scott, E.: The sexual offender. *Int J Offender Therapy and Comparative Criminology, 21*:255-263, 1977.

Scott, E.: The other side of the street: non-alcoholic adults from alcoholic homes. *Alcoholism Treatment Quarterly, 6*:63-74, 1989.

Scott, E.: Is there a criminal mind? *Int J Offender Therapy and Comparative Criminology, 33*:215-226, 1989.

Scott, E.: Prison group therapy with mentally and emotionally disturbed offenders. *Int J Offender Therapy and Comparative Criminology, 39*:131-145, 1993.

Scott, E.: Oedipus among prisoners? *Int J Offender Therapy and Comparative Criminology, 38*:277-280, 1994.

Scott, E.: When isn't a corpse dead? *Int J Offender Therapy and Comparative Criminology, 30*:3-4, 1996.

Scott, E.: Dionysus: Twice Born; and Criminals. *Int J Offender Therapy and Comparative Criminology, 40*:179-180, 1996.

Scott, E.: Group therapy with prisoners. In Palermo, G. and Scott, E. (Eds.): *The Paranoid: In and Out of Prison.* Springfield, Charles C. Thomas, 1997.

Shakespeare, W.: *MacBeth.* G. Hunter (Ed.). New York, Penguin, 1967.

Shakespeare, W.: *Hamlet.* E. Hubber (Ed.). New York, Signet Classic, 1963.

Seligman, M.: Science as an ally of practice. *Am Psychol, 51*:1072-1079, 1996.

Simon, R.: *Bad Men Do What Good Men Dream.* Washington, D.C., American Psychiatric Association, 1996.

Slavson, S.: *A Textbook in Analytic Group Psychotherapy.* New York, International Universities Press, 1964.

Sleek, S.: Bittersweet memories of study gone haywire. *Monitor,* October 1996, p. 8. American Psychological Association.

Slovenko, R.: *Psychiatry and Criminal Culpability.* New York, John Wiley & Sons, 1995.

Solomon, M.: *Mozart.* New York, Harper Pernial, 1995.

Sophocles: *Sophocles: The Oedipus Cycle.* English version by D. Fitts & R. Fitzgerald. New York, Harcourt Brace Jovanovich, 1971.

Spence, D.: *Narrative Truth and Historical Truth: Meaning and Interpretation in Psychoanalysis.* New York, W.W. Norton, 1984.

Sternberg, R. & Lubart, T.: Investing in creativity. *Am Psychol, 51*:677-688, 1996.

Stotland, E.: *The Psychology of Hope.* San Francisco, Jossey-Bass, 1969.

Symonds, P.: *Symonds Picture Story Test.* New York, Teachers College Press, 1948.

Talan, J.: New health villians: Anger and anxiety. *Oregonian,* June 5, p. A13, 1996.

Toch, H.: *Violent Men,* rev. ed. Washington, D.C., American Psychological Association, 1992.

Toch, H.: *Living in Prison.* Washington, D.C., American Psychological Association, 1992.

Van Voorhis, P.: *Psychological Classification of the Adult Male Prison Inmate.* Albany, State University of New York Press, 1994.

Vitz, P.: The use of stories in moral development. *Am Psych, 51*:667-688, 1990.

Walters, G.: The psychological inventory of criminal thinking styles: Part III: Prediction validity. *Int J Offender Therapy and Comparative Criminology, 40*:105-112, 1996.

Werge, T.: Mark Twain and America's soul. *Notre Dame Magazine:*13-17, 1984.

White, E.B.: *Essays of E.B. White,* 17th ed. New York, Harper Colophon, 1977.

Williams, M.: *The Velveteen Rabbit.* Philadelphia, Running Press, 1981.

Winnicott, D.: Transitional objects and transitional phenomena. *Int J Psycho-Analysis, 34*:89-97, 1953.

Winnicott, D.: Ego distortion in terms of true and false self. In *The Maturational Processes and the Facilitating Environment.* London, Hogarth Press, 1965, pp. 140-152.

Winnicott, D.: Playing: Its theoretical status in the clinical situation. *Int J Psycho-Analysis, 49*:591-598, 1968.

Zeanah, C., Anders, T., Seifer, R., & Stern, D.: Implications of research on infant development for psychodynamic theory and practice. *J Am Acad Child Adolescent Psychiatry, 28*:657-668, 1989.

NAME INDEX

A
Ablow, K., 141
Allen, J., 129
Andreasen, N., 27, 128
Anthony, J., 117, 120
Arieti, S., 30, 142
Azar, B., 109

B
Barth, K., 122
Baum, F., 49
Baumeister, B., 140
Bettelheim, B., 40, 45–47, 56, 58, 59, 67, 79, 144
Boethius, A., 61
Boorstin, D., 122
Bowlby, J., 36, 133, 134
Brown, R., 76, 92, 143

C
C'de Baca, J., 141
Carpenter, W., 28, 29
Chesterton, G. K., 117
Coles, R., 6, 141

D
Dies, R., 105
Dunne, J., 6, 24
Duvall, M., 119

E
Eisenberg, L., 27
Ellenberger, H., 30, 115, 141
Erikson, E., 23, 37, 148

F
Farley, F., 4, 148
Fine, R., 107
Frank, F., 106
Franz, C., 139
Freud, A., 5, 40

Freud, S., 23, 87, 116, 141, 144
Frost, R., 7, 19, 145

G
Gabbard, G., 25, 28, 126, 133
Guze, S., 26, 27

H
Halleck, S., 3
Hankoff, L., 126
Hatcher, E., 104, 119
Hawking, S., 143
Heuscher, J., 46, 47
Holton, C., 47
Huck, C., 47

K
Kagan, J., 143
Kay, J., 136
Kemker, S., 26, 27
Kinzie, D., 121

L
Lewis, L., 129
Lubart, T., 5, 144, 145
Ludwig, A., 31
Lynch, W., 75

M
Maslow, A., 23, 24, 37, 88, 130, 134, 145, 147
Mason, H., 92
May, R. 147
McAdams, D., 137, 139, 140
Meuller, G., 46
Miller, W., 141

P
Palmero, G., 4, 15, 24, 31, 34, 38
Peck, M., 141, 143
Peebles, M., 122, 126
Pipes, R., 142

Plato, 91, 103
Pontius, A., 129
Post, R., 21, 122, 129
Prins, H., 142
Pruyser, P., 29

R
Rennie, D., 6

S
Samenow, S., 9, 37
Sandler, J., 40
Satre, T., 142
Scott, E., 4, 5, 10, 15, 26, 31, 34, 36,
    38, 45, 46, 48, 79, 93, 103, 106, 111,
    113, 115, 127, 128, 133, 144
Self, 139
Seligman, M., 136, 137
Shakespeare, W., 6, 144
Simon, R., 141
Slavson, S., 107
Sleek, S., 107, 117
Slovenko, R., 25, 30, 141
Solomon, M., 63, 73, 77
Sophocles, 46
Spence, D., 6
Sternberg, R., 5, 144, 145
Stotland, E., 75
Strauss, J., 28, 29

T
Talan, J., 21
Toch, H., 9, 33, 34

V
Van Voorhis, P., 33
Vitz, P., 6

W
Werge, T., 122
White, E. B., 3
Williams, M., 45, 48, 76, 79, 144
Winnicott, D., 64, 117, 144

Z
Zeanah, C., 6, 139

SUBJECT INDEX

A

Adult Internal Management Systems (AIMS), 33
Agape, ix, 24
Altered state of consciousness, 16, 31, 119
    evil, 31–32
        prisoner dialogue, 31–32
    maladaptive and adaptive experiences, 31
Anger
    prisoner attitudes toward world, 20–21, 146
    prisoner dialogue, 18–19
    prisoner vignettes, 16–17
    stressors, 21–22
    trigger for sexual fantasies, 157
Assumptive world, 106
Axis I diagnosis, 12, 85
Axis II diagnosis, 4, 12

B

Brain
    biology, 27
    memory dynamics, 128–30
    prisoner vignette, 28
    social structure, 27–29

C

Card B9 (see Symonds Test)
Central nervous system, 28–29
Chemical imbalance, 27
Chronic psychological stress, 28–29
Clinical messages
    changing assumptions, 106
    group therapy dynamics and structure, 105–19
    metanoia, to turn around, 32, 106
    response to the good efforts of prison therapy, 5
    talk it out, don't act it out, 10, 38, 107
Conception (own)
    prisoner dialogue, 99–100
Conceptual Level, 33
Consumer Reports, mental health survey results, 136–37
Correctional psychologist (*see* Psychologist, correctional)
Creativity, 5, 88, 144–45
    Maslow's two types, 88
Crime fixation, 40, 135
Crystallization of discontent, 140

D

Death
    PET responses, 38
Dialogues
    anger, 18–19
    conception, 99–100
    homicide, 25–26
    inmost heart, 12–14, 28
    sexual victimization, 94
    world, 20–21, 146
Don't want to tell; want to tell, 41
    PET responses, 41–42
Dreams, 67, 87, 144
DSM-IV, 4, 12, 23, 25, 27, 30, 88, 121
Dual diagnosis, 12, 81

E

Ego-dystonic, 107
Ego-syntonic, 107
Emotions
    anger dialogue, 18–19
    disturbed emotions, 9
    heart connotations, 10–12
    kardia, 25
    love, 23–24
        eros vs. agape, 24

negative emotions, 9
type groupings of inmost heart feelings, 15
Eros, ix, 24
Evil, 25, 30, 141–44
    altered state of consciousness, 31
    Arieti's summary, 142
    British review of literature, 30
    dream's navel, 144
    DSM-IV exclusion, 25, 30, 141
    fairy tale presentation, 47
    psychotic vs. religious mystical states, 30

F
Fables, 47
Fairy tales
    change of mind or heart, responses, 49–50, 52–53, 55–56
    distinctions from fables, 47
    Greek myths, clinical utilization, 45–46, 57, 79
    imprisonment, effects of long-term, 56–59
    real or mechanical, responses, 48–49, 51–52, 54–55
    utilization with prisoners, 47–59
Fairy tales, written by prisoners, 61–77
Fantasy
    sexual activity, 93
    sexual offender's story of fantasy and acting out, 156–57
    tutored fantasy, 29
Fisherman and the Genie, clinical application, 56–59

G
Genetic loading, 27
God
    PET responses, 37–38
Group therapy (*see also* Clinical messages)
    action-oriented, 105
    anger dialogue, 18–19
    ego-dystonic, ego-syntonic orientation, 107
    fairy tales, clinical utilization, 47–59
    Greek myths, clinical utilization, 45–46
    inmost heart, 12–14, 28
    interpersonal, 105
    prison setting, vii, 10, 108–19
    population classifications, 108
    psychodynamic, 105
    sexual activity, 91–97
        own conception, 97–102
Group therapy techniques, 108–19
    diaper, 111–12
    disclosure of one's own story, 110, 139–40
    dream task, 111, 113–15
    freedom to disagree, 110
    humor, 110, 116
    play and playfulness, 116–19
    psychodrama, 111
    psychologist's observation and feedback, 108
    symbolism and reality, 112
    talk it out; don't act it out, 10, 38, 107
    technical neutrality, 110
Guilt, 40

H
Happiness and self-judgement, 5
Hate, 26
Heart
    emotional groupings, 15
    emotional terminology, 10–12
    kardia, 25
    prison group responses to inmost heart question, 12–14, 28
Homicide, 25–26, 53

I
Illusionistic world, 29
Individual maturation, xiii
Interpersonal Maturity Level, 33

J
Jesness Inventory, 33

K
Kardia, 25 (*see also* Heart)
Kindling, 122, 129–30, 134

L
Life narrative disclosure of one's own story, 110, 139–40
Love
    civilizing factor, 23
    dearth of scholarly references, 23
    expression toward mother, 37
    love and be loved, 23–24, 130–33
    loving lessons, 146–48

narcissism, 37, 145
PET responses, 37, 130–33, 145

M

Memory, 128–34
  episodic, 128
  free association, 128
  randomepisodic silent thinking (REST), 128–29
  semantic, 128
Metanoia, 32
MMPI, 33
Mythology
  confrontational, xi
  Eros and Aphrodite, 24

N

Narrative self, 6, 139–40
  interchange of narrative and historical truth, 6
  story within a story, 6
Noncompliance, 27

O

Offenders (*see also* Prisoners)
  anger
    prisoner dialogue, 18–19
    prisoner vignettes, 16–17
  change of mind or heart, responses, 49–50, 52–53, 55–56
  groupings of inmost heart emotions, 15
  imprisonment, effects of long-term, 56–59
  inmost heart, 12–14, 28
  loving lessons, 146–48
  psychological classifications, 33
  real or mechanical, responses, 48–49, 51–52, 54–55
  statistical success with therapy, 3
  thinking styles, 33
  vignettes, 28

P

Personality
  level 1, traits, 137
  level 2, personal concerns, motivations 138
  level 3, life narrative, 139–40
  prisoner vignettes, 137, 138
Personality disorder, 81
PET (*see* Prison Expression Test)

Play and playfulness in group therapy, 116–19
Post Growth Experience (PGE), ix, 5, 121–28, 133
  definition, 122
  prisoner responses to positive event question, 123–26
  proactive techniques, 122
Post Traumatic Stress Disorder (PTSD), ix, 5, 121–28, 133
  childhood experiences, 126–28
  definition, 121
  study of diagnosed, 133
Prison
  psychological cleansing, vii
Prison Expression Test (PET), ix, 4, 33–43, 149–52, 153–55
  construction, 34
    testing results, 34–43
    text, 149–52, 153–55
Prison Preference Inventory (PPI), ix, 34
Prison terminology
  pump-primer, 5
  riding a bum beef, 5, 15
  stand-up man, 5, 48, 113
Prisoner-cancer, 19
Prisoners (*see also* Offenders)
  anger
    prisoner dialogue, 18–19
    prisoner vignettes, 16–17
  change of mind or heart, responses, 49–50, 52–53, 55–56
  conception responses, 99–100
  fairy tales, written by prisoners, 61–77
  imprisonment, effects of long-term, 56–59
  inmost heart, 12–14, 28
  groupings of inmost heart emotions, 15
  psychological classifications, 33
  real or mechanical, responses, 48–49, 51–52, 54–55
  statistical success with therapy, 3
  Symonds Test, Card B9 stories, 80–89
  thinking styles, 33
  vignettes, 28
  unhappy background, 134
Psychiatric swearing, xiii
Psychological classifications of prisoners, 33
Psychologist, correctional

emotional insulation, viii, 3
professional struggles, viii
stamina, 3
timing, importance, 10

R
Randomepisodic silent thinking (REST), 128–29
Recidivism
    impact of post-prison work, viii
Remorse, 40
Rewriting of self stories, 5

S
Self, stages
    fifth stage, narrative self, 6
    self-reflection, PET responses, 42
Self-injury phenomenon, 19
Sex, 4, 39, 91–102
    activity, group therapy, 93–97
    child molestation, 94
    conception (self) knowledge, 97–102
    crime fixation, 40
    PET responses, 39–40
    phallic fixation, 40
    sexual offenders and fantasy, 93
Sexual activity, historical literature overview, 92–93
Solipsism, viii
Symond's Test, 79

T
Thematic Apperception Test (TAT), 140
Therapy (*see* Group therapy)
Transitional object, 64

V
Velveteen Rabbit, clinical application, 45–56
Victim identity, 5, 7, 38, 105
PET responses, 38–39

W
Working alliance criteria, 10

Z
Zimbardo's simulation of prison interaction, 106–7

CHARLES C THOMAS • PUBLISHER, LTD.

- Everstine, Louis—THE ANATOMY OF SUICIDE: Silence of the Heart. '98, 170 pp. (7 x 10), 6 il., $42.95, cloth, $27.95, paper.

- Oehlert, Mary E., Scott Sumerall & Shane J. Lopez—INTERNSHIP SELECTION IN PROFESSIONAL PSYCHOLOGY: A Comprehensive Guide for Students, Faculty, and Training Directors. '98, 172 pp. (7 x 10), 3 tables, $42.95, cloth, $27.95, paper.

- Perticone, Eugene X.—THE CLINICAL AND PROJECTIVE USE OF THE BENDER-GESTALT TEST. '98, 160 pp. (7 x 10), 45 il.

- Hall, C. Margaret—HEROIC SELF: Sociological Dimensions of Clinical Practice. '98, 140 pp. (7 x 10).

- Frostig, Karen & Michele Essex—EXPRESSIVE ARTS THERAPIES IN SCHOOLS: A Supervision and Program Development Guide. '98, 136 pp. (8 1/2 x 11), 8 il., spiral (paper).

- Feder, Bernard & Elaine Feder—THE ART AND SCIENCE OF EVALUATION IN THE ARTS THERAPIES: How Do You Know What's Working? '98, 350 pp. (7 x 10), 25 il.

- Benenzon, Rolando O.—MUSIC THERAPY THEORY AND MANUAL: Contributions to the Knowledge of Nonverbal Contexts. (2nd Ed.) '97, 296 pp. (7 x 10), 44 il., $59.95, cloth, $44.95, paper.

- Kelly, Francis D.—THE CLINICAL INTERVIEW OF THE ADOLESCENT: From Assessment and Formulation to Treatment Planning. '97, 234 pp. (7 x 10), 2 tables, $59.95, cloth, $45.95, paper.

- Walsh, William M. & G. Robert Williams—SCHOOLS AND FAMILY THERAPY: Using Systems Theory and Family Therapy in the Resolution of School Problems. '97, 236 pp. (7 x 10), 2 il., 5 tables, $47.95, cloth, $34.95, paper.

- Crow, Gary A. & Letha I. Crow—HELPING PARENTS COPE WITH CHILDREN'S ADJUSTMENT PROBLEMS: An Advice-Giving Guide for Professionals. '97, 122 pp. (7 x 10), $31.95, cloth, $21.95, paper.

- Spencer, Linda Bushell—HEAL ABUSE AND TRAUMA THROUGH ART: Increasing Self-Worth, Healing of Initial Wounds, and Creating a Sense of Connectivity. '97, 250 pp. (7 x 10), 10 il., $59.95, cloth, $39.95, paper.

- Blank, Leonard—CHANGING BEHAVIOR IN INDIVIDUALS, COUPLES, AND GROUPS: Identifying, Analyzing and Manipulating the Elements Involved in Change in Order to Promote or Inhibit Alteration of Behavior. '96, 202 pp. (7 x 10), 1 il., $44.95, cloth, $28.95, paper.

- Moon, Bruce L.—ART AND SOUL: Reflections on an Artistic Psychology. '96, 156 pp. (7 x 10), 15 il., $36.95, cloth, $25.95, paper.

- Anderson, Robert M., Jr., Terri L. Needels & Harold V. Hall—AVOIDING ETHICAL MISCONDUCT IN PSYCHOLOGY SPECIALTY AREAS. '98, 340 pp. (7 x 10).

- Parker, Woodrow M.—CONSCIOUSNESS-RAISING: A Primer for Multicultural Counseling. (2nd Ed.) '98, 328 pp. (7 x 10), 2 il., 3 tables, $62.95, cloth, $47.95, paper.

- Malouff, John & Nicola Schutte—GAMES TO ENHANCE SOCIAL AND EMOTIONAL SKILLS: Sixty-Six Games that Teach Children, Adolescents, and Adults Skills Crucial to Success in Life. '98, 218 pp. (8 1/2 x 11), 3 il., spiral (paper), $33.95.

- Brunstetter, Richard W.—ADOLESCENTS IN PSYCHIATRIC HOSPITALS: A Psychodynamic Approach to Evaluation and Treatment. '98, 180 pp. (7 x 10).

- Fairchild, Thomas N.—CRISIS INTERVENTION STRATEGIES FOR SCHOOL-BASED HELPERS. (2nd Ed.) '97, 496 pp. (7 x 10), 8 il., 12 tables, $109.95, cloth, $92.95, paper.

- Laban, Richard J.—CHEMICAL DEPENDENCY TREATMENT PLANNING HANDBOOK. '97, 174 pp. (8 1/2 x 11), $29.95, spiral (paper).

- Hammer, Emanuel F.—ADVANCES IN PROJECTIVE DRAWING INTERPRETATION. '97, 476 pp. (7 x 10), 202 il., 8 tables, $95.95, cloth, $69.95, paper.

- Schlesinger, Louis B. & Eugene Revitch—SEXUAL DYNAMICS OF ANTI-SOCIAL BEHAVIOR. (2nd Ed.) '97, 324 pp. (7 x 10), 4 il., 2 tables, $64.95, cloth, $49.95, paper.

- Love, Harold D.—CHARACTERISTICS OF THE MILDLY HANDICAPPED: Assisting Teachers, Counselors, Psychologists, and Families to Prepare for Their Roles in Meeting the Needs of the Mildly Handicapped in a Changing Society. '97, 210 pp. (7 x 10), 13 il., 22 tables, $44.95, cloth, $29.95, paper.

- Radocy, Rudolf E. & J. David Boyle—PSYCHOLOGICAL FOUNDATIONS OF MUSICAL BEHAVIOR. (3rd Ed.) '97, 408 pp. (7 x 10), 9 il., 3 tables, $61.95, cloth, $44.95, paper.

- Schlesinger, Louis B.—EXPLORATIONS IN CRIMINAL PSYCHOPATHOLOGY: Clinical Syndromes with Forensic Implications. '96, 366 pp. (7 x 10), 2 il., 10 tables, $77.95, cloth, $51.95, paper.

- Plach, Tom—THE CREATIVE USE OF MUSIC IN GROUP THERAPY. (2nd Ed.) '96, 84 pp. (7 x 10), $31.95, cloth, $20.95 paper.

- Weikel, William J. & Artis J. Palmo—FOUNDATIONS OF MENTAL HEALTH COUNSELING. (2nd Ed.) '96, 446 pp. (7 x 10), 7 il., 1 table, $89.95, cloth, $68.95, paper.

Write, call 1-800-258-8980 or 1-217-789-8980 or FAX (217)789-9130 • www.ccthomas.com • books@ccthomas.com
Books sent on approval • $5.50 - Shipping / $6.50 - Canada • Prices subject to change without notice

2600 South First Street • Springfield • Illinois • 62704